A Poetry of Remembrance

MARY BURRITT CHRISTIANSEN POETRY SERIES
V. B. PRICE, SERIES EDITOR

Mary Burritt
Christiansen
Poetry Series

Also available in the University of New Mexico Press
Mary Burritt Christiansen Poetry Series:

Poets of the Non-Existent City: Los Angeles in the McCarthy Era
edited by Estelle Gershgoren Novak

Selected Poems of Gabriela Mistral edited by Ursula K. Le Guin

Deeply Dug In by R. L. Barth

Amulet Songs: Poems Selected and New by Lucile Adler

In Company: An Anthology of New Mexico Poets After 1960
edited by Lee Bartlett, V. B. Price, and Dianne Edenfield Edwards

Tiempos Lejanos: Poetic Images from the Past
by Nasario García

Refuge of Whirling Light by Mary Beath

The River Is Wide/El río es ancho: Twenty Mexican Poets,
a Bilingual Anthology
edited and translated by Marlon L. Fick

A Scar Upon Our Voice by Robin Coffee

CrashBoomLove: A Novel in Verse by Juan Felipe Herrera

In a Dybbuk's Raincoat: Collected Poems by Bert Meyers

Rebirth of Wonder: Poems of the Common Life
by David M. Johnson

Broken and Reset: Selected Poems, 1966 to 2006 by V. B. Price

The Curvature of the Earth
by Gene Frumkin and Alvaro Cardona-Hine

Derivative of the Moving Image by Jennifer Bartlett

Map of the Lost by Miriam Sagan

¿de Veras?: Young Voices from the National Hispanic Cultural Center
edited by Mikaela Jae Renz and Shelle VanEtten-Luaces

A Bigger Boat: The Unlikely Success of the Albuquerque Poetry Slam Scene
edited by Susan McAllister, Don McIver, Mikaela Renz, and Daniel Solis

Pasó por Aquí
Series on the Nuevomexicano Literary Heritage
Edited by Genaro M. Padilla, Erlinda Gonzales-Berry,
and A. Gabriel Meléndez

A POETRY

of REMEMBRANCE

New and Rejected Works

LEVI ROMERO

Foreword by V. B. Price

Preface by Rudolfo Anaya

Afterword by Genaro M. Padilla

University of New Mexico Press

Albuquerque

© 2008 by the University of New Mexico Press
All rights reserved. Published 2008
Printed in the United States of America
First paperbound printing, 2009
Paperbound ISBN: 978-0-8263-4510-3

15 14 13 12 11 10 09   1 2 3 4 5 6 7

Library of Congress Cataloging-in-Publication Data

Romero, Levi.
A poetry of remembrance : new and rejected works / Levi Romero.
        p. cm. — (Mary Burritt Christiansen poetry series)
Poems in English and Spanish.
ISBN 978-0-8263-4509-7 (alk. paper)
I. Title.
PS3568.O56444P64 2008
811'.54—dc22

                        2008028669

Designed and typeset by Mina Yamashita.
Text composed in Minion Pro, display font in Brioso Pro,
both designed by Robert Slimbach for Adobe.
Printed by Thomson-Shore, Inc. on 55# Natures Natural.

this is for Jeana,

Jeana, this is for you

Se ha usado el idioma del norte de Nuevo México

Contents

Foreword

INTIMATE, INCLUSIVE, LINGUISTICALLY INTRIGUING, *A Poetry of Remembrance: New and Rejected Works* by Levi Romero is both a poetic lens through which to explore metaphors of New Mexico's inner life and a passionate book of candor and nostalgia that openheartedly embraces the world. Using New Mexican Spanish and English, Romero's poems expand both languages, allowing them to open to one another and enrich the opportunities for cultural exchange and exploration.

Some of the poems in this book are largely in New Mexican Spanish; many poems in English have metaphors and references in New Mexican Spanish and even bilingual puns. Monolingual readers might normally be put off by this interpenetration of languages. And while it might serve readers well to have a Spanish-language dictionary with them, preferably *A Dictionary of New Mexico and Southern Colorado Spanish* by Rubén Cobos, Romero's genius for communication takes all the pain out of translation. I'm not sure how he does this, but for a person like myself who has struggled with Spanish and who considers himself New Mexican in his soul, if not in his lineage, Romero's poetry is so welcoming and so humane that a second language becomes not a code for exclusion, but a map of recognition and community.

Romero was born and raised in farming country in the Embudo Valley of northern New Mexico, between Taos and Santa Fe. Wonderful passages in these poems describe his younger years as a lowrider, cruiser in Española in the early 1970s. In "Lowcura: An Introspective *Virtual Cruise* Through an American Subcultural Tradition," he describes going with his cousins to "Espa', usually cruising with my cousin Raymond in his dropped 1955 Chevy pickup truck. It was a beautiful piece of nostalgia painted a Diamond Black, rolling on baby-moon chromed rims on gangster-wide whitewall tires, with hood mounted dummy spotlights and Bob Dylan on his stereo."

Just as many New Mexicans are polylingual, many poets and writers, everywhere in the world, find out through tough circumstances that they are poly-gifted and blessed with wide-reaching curiosities. Levi Romero apprenticed early as a draftsman and a builder, became an architect, taught creative writing at the University of New Mexico, and, through independent workshops and other venues, helps writers of every age and background find the confidence they need to make work and perform it. He is currently a visiting Research Scholar in the School of Architecture and Planning at UNM, focusing on architectural and cultural landscapes studies.

In the Taos Summer Writers' Conference in 2006, for instance, Romero offered a workshop in bilingual poetry, asking students to write their own autobiographical poems. Romero focused the workshop on "encouraging bilingualism by bringing both teachers' and students' cultures into the classroom," he wrote. "By offering culturally diverse literature, teachers reflect and honor the many cultures in the classroom. Bilingual poetry can encourage the development of voice, reflection, and identity through the use of language. . . ." One of his teaching strategies, he writes, is to show that "the point of poetry is articulation and clarity."

That view is reflected beautifully in his own work. In the poem "Diablitos," a term his mother used to describe dragonflies, Romero moves through the talk of death and dying with his mother,

> it's something we've only talked about occasionally
> in that loose form of broken structure
> and resolution
>
> working its way toward nothing
> reaching for itself

in that final gesture
and calculated language
that finds itself

    woven and looped
    up and under
    in and out
    until it's made its way
    through and through
    to the other end

a tapestry of the said and unsaid
of the thought about too much
    and of
        the dared
            not even
                think

what can one say?

Writers who have suffered because their art doesn't fit neatly into the American literati template can understand and appreciate Romero's take on the American literary establishment.

In the poem "New and Rejected Works," Romero writes about "a dropped/metallic lavender colored '66 LeMans" and asks

what true literary aficionado
could understand or bare even the slightest interest
in this ghost-patterned paint, chrome and rubber observation?

will this poem
be allowed to exist
alongside other genres of poetry?

to say the least of its highly improbable publication possibilities
in reputable, established "American" literary journals
that hold, in their editorial exercising power
the ability to affirm and measure
a writer's worthwhile poetic existence
no, probably not

yet, that bumper scraping cruiser
dressed in accessories from a past era
and cruising down the street literally naked
to the general public mind
was nothing but *pura poesía* to me

In the poem "Taos Nicho," Romero opens his poetic conscience to reenactments of the history of New Mexico, rejoicing and lamenting:

and I am everything at that point

and nothing

for I could feel joyous and celebratory
for we have endured

my people
mi raza
el mestizaje

la huerfandad

the orphaned ones
whom Spain abandoned
Mexico did not adopt
and the U.S. never wanted

and i feel the sorrow of the *Indio*

because of that
            enduring

The poems of Levi Romero strengthen my sense of place in New Mexico, not only because they speak to what Romero has characterized as the "manito culture of northern New Mexico and our experiences as people subjected to the threat of cultural displacement within our own homeland," but because they speak with the human heart in all of us as we connect with the loyalty and devotion to the land around us and to the families, children, and friends we cherish above all others. As readers do with poets who become the friends of their inner lives through the magic of Orpheus, many readers will find, as I have, a home in Levi Romero's work.

—V. B. Price
Albuquerque, New Mexico

Preface

LEVI ROMERO is heir to an artistic movement that has come to be known as the Embudo Renaissance. Embudo, New Mexico, also known as Dixon, New Mexico, lies in a valley north of Española on the road to Taos. At that confluence the Embudo River flows into the Rio Grande, which comes roaring out of the gorge.

The Embudo Valley is a hundreds-of-years-old homeland to the Españoles-mexicanos who settled there. Ages of history run in the Embudo earth. The valley grows delicious apples, peaches, and garden produce, the food of *la gente*: corn, chile, tomatoes, other vegetables. Organic, the hippies of the '60s called the food. They also found Embudo to be Nirvana.

La gente, the hispanos, have persisted. They have been in those valleys too long to be moved by fads. Organic? "*Pues*, we been eating organic for five hundred years. *Y qué?*"

In the 1960s and into the '70s the Embudo Renaissance was a gathering of poets, academics, farmers, *vatos*, *plebe*, and lowriders. They gathered in this circle of culture to mine what they called "*el oro del barrio*." Not gold in the hills, but the *sabiduria* (knowledge) of la gente. This young group of very talented vatos gathered to create a revolution. Their ancestors had survived five hundred years in those valleys: la gente knew something of survival and creativity.

So they gathered not in Chicago or L.A., but right there in their ancestral home ground. Their educational forums produced a renaissance in the same way any gathering of artists and philosophers creates new paradigms from the materials of their history and culture. They knew the knowledge of the ancestors, el oro del barrio, could and must function in present-day reality.

I know a few of the participants of the Embudo Renaissance. Tomas Atencio taught that learning best takes place in the forum, the agora. Liberation Pablo Freire style. Dialogue. Listen to la gente.

They know what's good in life; they also know oppression. Later he taught at the University of New Mexico; Tomas remains one of the most important New Mexican sociologists/philosophers of our time.

E. A. Mares, Tony, was part of the group. A brilliant mind, also a teacher and one of our finest poets. His range of interests is incredible.

Estevan Arellano, who lives in Embudo, is a talented artist—his home is a gallery. Estevan has researched the original farming techniques of his ancestors and now teaches classes on the process. Multitalented, he has also been a publisher and activist.

All were activists. They formed el oro del barrio and found the knowledge of la gente, and they spread the word, informing us of the role liberation and creativity play in our lives.

During that time Levi Romero was a rebellious young man, not well understood in the classrooms where he turned in his poetry instead of book reviews, wore long hair, answered questions about Shakespeare in Spanish instead of the Queen's English, stayed up late drawing instead of studying, and was lowriding by age twelve.

He felt the oppression so many of la gente were feeling. "*Qué chingao está* happening to my gente?" he asked. "Born free but in chains! *Qué pasó?* Our own history no longer ours."

So he showed up and listened to those early seminars of the Embudo Renaissance.

The language of the Nuevo Mexicanos is full of metaphors, and as a metaphorical language it is a poetic language. Levi grew up steeped in the language of *el norte*, the Rio Arriba gente. Language is the hallmark of his poetic strength. The *cuentos, dichos, adivinanzas, refranes*, prayers, *alabados, los vatos torriquiando*, all fed Levi's imagination, as did the '60s and '70s lowrider lingo. Levi speaks and writes the *español* of la gente: English, Spanglish, lowrider, *calo, chuco, y lineas* (lines) from his training as an architect.

(As a boy growing up in the Embudo Valley Levi must have been in awe of the curves of adobe walls, shadows, form, shape, weight, buttresses, vigas, mud becoming adobe in forms, straw, *mujeres enjarando*, and the voices of the men and women who worked the mud into adobe. Levi heard the voices in the earth. Forms spoke. The voices led him to dream and become an architect, and so his poetic lines are full of architectural allusions. The architect of mud. Zoquete.)

In one poem he uses an old dicho: "*Todos quieren la gloria, pero nadien quiere la cruz*." The metaphor is worth a preacher's hour-long sermon or a daylong seminar by the poets and thinkers of the Embudo Renaissance. That rich metaphorical language of la gente is Levi's inheritance. Today the young seem to know much about *quantity*: numbers and amount. They no longer use the language of metaphors.

Levi was listening and rubbing elbows with the most important creative impulse to come out of New Mexico in the last hundred years. The creativity of the Embudo Renaissance is still alive and well, witness Levi's poetry. Levi uses the language of metaphor to evoke the power of memory and family traditions.

Levi's poem "Diablitos" is one of the most powerful poems in praise of a mother (his mother rests half-dazed in a nursing home) that I have ever read. Here the poet sets the stage for the major theme of this collection: evoking memory, which also means evoking the imagination and the particular muses of time and place. The *duende* is alive in the poems! The *duende está bien loco*! The duende often dresses as a lowrider! Or as a humble paisano expressing the profound joy and sadness of *la vida triste*.

At the end Levi closes with "El veintinueve de agosto" where he again visits his mother. These visits to the nursing home frame the collection. "El veintinueve de agosto" drives a nail into the heart of the reader. The mother remembers the past, la gente, *vecinos*, customs, history. She admonishes the poet (Levi) to *remember*. And so poetry is a remembering. *La vida pronto se acaba*. Remembering is the most powerful muse after all.

These two poems deserve to be anthologized far and wide.

But there's more poetry between beginning and end. Here we find not only a looking back, but the struggle of the poet to find his voice. He reads the Chicano poets of the Chicano Movimiento. In boarding school he reads Montoya's "El Louie." He goes on to read Raul Salinas and other rebels of the movement. Their concerns become Levi's concerns. Their voices from the barrios and prisons instill in him the desire to sing his poems in his own unique voice.

Everyday intimate events and people are *chispas* that spark the poem. Levi reveals family life and teenage years, in rhythmic Spanish and in-your-face bilingual Spanglish—all levels of language serve the poet. Levi's duende spirit is restless, and it smolders with true poetic intent.

Lowrider poems slip into *puro manito* Spanish/Spanglish with words not found in the Velasquez dictionary. Writing poetry is lowriding/lowcura. He searches for his identity. "De donde yo soy" echoes Corky's "Yo Soy Joaquin." The Anglo-American culture of the classroom was covering el oro del barrio with lead. La plebe was losing its sense of identity. It was time to melt away the lead to reveal el oro. These are poems of revelation.

The struggle for cultural survival was brewing, and Levi was to play a key role in that struggle. "Molino abandonado" is but one of the poems that addresses the urgent need to reconnect to our history and culture.

There's much more in this collection. The spiritual essence of the Rio Grande corridor and its tributaries shines in every poem. From the loco to the sublime, Levi's poems are a blessing on our heads.

—Rudolfo Anaya
Albuquerque, New Mexico

I.

Holding my ear to your words

today, as always

Dear Judyth,

a few poems

it has been in death that we have learned how to live
the reduction of all so much
down to a few words

i put this package together as i prepared breakfast
if it smells like frying bacon
and the warmth of saturday morning
and sounds like daughters laughing, dogs barking
and looks like the sight of crumpled, unmade beds
and stacks up like the dirty laundry pile growing evermore fervently

it is a good sign

a sign that does not
indicate *yield* or *stop*
but *go*

and go and go and go!

got a card yesterday
from a couple i taught
in a workshop
several years ago

they said their memories
of me
and their fondness of which

had inspired them to name
their newborn son
after me

so now
in Minneapolis
in the wintry spell
of another new year
and a life beginning

one day too, it may be asked
Mom, how did i get my name?

and it will be remembered

Diablitos

¡ay, ay, mamá!

this morning
the dragonflies
were fluttering above the pond

diablitos

diablitos, you used to call them

yesterday at the nursing home

your hair
tied up in a bun
rouge applied to your cheeks by the attendant

a dab of color to keep the day
cheerful and young

I had never seen your hair
done that way before
you were always so stubborn
that years ago you would not have allowed it so

these days
your hair in a bun
and your stories once long and complete

fragmented
with no beginning
no middle
and no end

good poems all

in that way

and how much longer
    I wonder
before even they are gone

before
you
leave
us
alone and fluttering

our reflections rippling against the water
our auras settled across the meadow

in
colors
of
the
dragonfly

nomás Dios sabe cuándo, mijito
you've said on occasion

    death and dying

    it's something we've only talked about occasionally
    in that loose form of broken structure
    and resolution

working its way toward nothing
reaching for itself

in that final gesture
and calculated language
that finds itself

woven and looped
up and under
in and out
until it's made its way
through and through
to the other end

a tapestry of the said and unsaid
of the thought about too much
and of
the dared
not even
think

what can one say?

death life living dying

you tell a story

that I find difficult to follow
and when you laugh
at midsentence

I try hard to keep with
the story line
and how it goes from

a that
   to
a this

but I realize
that I've missed it again

years ago I would've thought
that it was you
   and how
you might've spun your story
in a way that left
the listener confused

the punch line coming in
at midparagraph

but I see now
that it's been
   me
   us
   a world
   around you

that didn't quite catch
the inside joke
the developing story line

the drama
the mystery
the humor
the character unfolding
you had it all along, mom

the poetry

at the nursing home yesterday
the multicolored hairpins on your head
settled like dragonflies
sprouted like the dandelions
on the hillside

the sound
the reflection
the aura
the fluorescence

your voice

your tongue plopping against your bare gums
like the sound of a pebble
cast into the pond

you who never commanded an audience
by intention
    or so I thought

holding my ear
    to your words
    today as always

    la Mary Schwartz
    andava embolada y llegó a la media noche
    a mi puerta, casi desnuda y cayéndose

and then you break out into laughter

at midsentence

between the sounds of a patient
down the corridor
screaming in a language
that I can't understand

¿verdad?

   you ask, nudging me

     just to make sure that
     I'm following along

     mm hmm, así es, mamá
        así es

but, I know I've missed it
     again

mamá, a qué mamá

the poetry and the verse
between the laughter
   and
     the
       sunlight

prisms of color dancing
     ¡diablitos!

¡mira, mamá, mira
   los diablitos!

Capulín

at the Wal-Mart pharmacy in Española
a woman's prescription costs $400.00
causing a stir of *ooohs* and *aahs*
among those standing in line

it's for my son, she says
he needs three injections a day
insulin? someone asks
no, to thin out his blood

¡remedios!

someone in line blurts out the word
everyone agrees

yuh, mm hmm
remedios

yuh, remedios would be better and cheaper
capulín, chokecherry! someone remarks
my grandmother used to say that chokecherry
was good for thinning the blood

another woman adds,
the bark from the chokecherry tree, boiled into a tea,
or you can make the jam syrupy, drippy

más antes salía uno a los barrancos y jallaba uno de todito

we jostle ourselves from foot to foot mumbling

our memories

past lessons learned and rekindled
a greater wisdom priceless and an offered prescription
for lost traditions and discarded remedies

at Wal-Mart

Primito

me ladié acá Primito
allí en Velarde
a ese patio de aquella estación
al fin cerrada por el siempre

a escribir estas líneas
> lo que se discutió
> entre dos paisanos
> al oír mi voz en el radio

tiene el sonidito
> *¿cuál sonidito?*
el sonidito aquel
> *¿cómo?*
aquel sonidito
de los Romeros

¿y quién supiera mejor que él
> de ese sonidito?

el que vio a los Romeros nacer
el que vio a los Romeros morir

> ya los que eran
> no son
> y los que son
> no están
> y los que están
> no hay
> y los que hay
> no va a haber

¡ay, Primito!

necesito un galón de aceite de lámpara
¿qué tanto por un saco de carbón?
échele cinco de regulár

¿le falta medio cuarto?

bueno, thank you, eh
y vuelvan otra vez
saludes a la parentela

bueno, Primito, gracias
y ahi nos vemos

las gasolineras; ni seña
la compresora; asoleada, verde,
con la faja suelta y rajada
nada de aquel tsst, tsst, tsst, tsst
llantas pelonas, arrimadas en contra de la pader
los resolaneros; ni sombra, ni juellas, paisa

nada quedó
nada quedó

el sonidito

el silencio

Dear Ulysses

the library shelves here at the state mental hospital
are filled with the sort of books
that as a child you might've loved to read

they are marked between the loose pages
of a memory back stepping with a haunting humor
to those adolescent years you spent flipping
through nervous rhyme

but, dear Ulysses
you are not going to put away
this afternoon's watercolor project
for a bit of Zora

and your two-pack-a-day cigarette habit
is not going to blow itself into a cloud
that you can thumbly smudge away

on that winter's day years ago
when you stood naked at the iced edge of the stream
the idea, you said, was to swim underwater
upstream against the current and not even make a splash
the way fish do it!, you confidently remarked
as you yanked your socks off and plunged in

this afternoon the hollow tuba voices down the corridor
sound as strung out as an untuned symphony
while you laugh, observing how we look so much like men now
men, yes, men already

was it not just yesterday
the stiff prick of adolescence
saluted life to come?
it came
and here you are
describing your four suicide attempts
while the rain outside drizzles
in soft brushstrokes across the field

I imagine how you might've run and dived off the hospital roof
your arms rigidly set against your body
your toes extended outward
how you would've calculated your arc in a manner
so that you'd hit the surface of the pavement below head on
no belly flop for you, dear Ulysses

but a beautiful swimmer's dive
clean and precise

today, we grasp for a link back
to rocking cribs, family outings
and your mama's Southern lullabies

we say good-bye
to Christmastime ping-pong parlor games
and to woodstove crackling
and nut-cracking conversations
over hot apple cider, good night to nighttime
at the kitchen table art projects
splattered with Van Goghish colors
across the wet crumpled page

you are alone
alone
without the pass
without the key

the bars across these windows
are hard and cold
my old friend
cold on this day raining

and neither this morning's meadowlark's purr
nor your plucking of the sunny dandelion's petals
will free your mind's playful tricks
of *she loves me yes, she loves me not*

dear Ulysses, dear Ulysses

A Tender Willow

next to the pasture field
where the willows are again thick
and overgrown

it was there where he had planned to build their home

clearing hard for a life ahead and beyond
and not even time would tell
what it could be like

 a family
 a home
 a young love
and growing old

together

I remember
almost as if it never happened
a reminiscence resigned to imagination
like the farthest

farthest of memories

he wore his hair long
and he was still youthfully thin
his skin darkened by the sun
in that new spring

his young body bent
shirtless and dampened
sweat like alfalfa dew
clearing the stones, axing the wood

the graduation receptions
had already been celebrated
his girlfriend working through her new summer job

sixteen years later
at his funeral, she stood aside
holding a picture she had kept of him

a tender willow
young and strong
against the wind

Off've Central

back home
back then
even now
there are certain connotations conjured up
just by the mere mention of

Central

main street Alburqué
that portion of
scruffy dog tail laid out
just below the scraggly Sandias
and east of the thirsting Rio Puerco

Central

the granddaughter descendant of Route 66

Central

back home a hundred and thirty miles upstream
men regarded it with

curiosity
contempt
disdain
humor and desire

¡una puta bien hecha!

the red-light district
embedded into memories
of late adolescent mischievous rides
into Alburqué

cuentos of what happened
on a trip into town on an errand to pick up
an overhauled engine exchange
or something like that

¿iii, te acuerdas?

tales of what could be bought
indiscriminately, conveniently
twenty dollars for this
sixty dollars for that

so when as a young boy
Chente asked his older sister,
who was home visiting from the University,
where it was abouts that she lived
and she replied

off've Central

it startled him

and in the presence of his friend
felt the implications forming
the name calling
the teasing

Vicente's sister lives off've Central,
Vicente's sister lives off've Central

he imagined the recess circles of accusation
heard the bully choir singing
saw the after-school specials
being notched out on the calendar
and no known way to avoid them

he thought about it hard

later, he walked his friend out
to the arroyo
looked him in his eyes
and instructed him

don't-cha tell anyone, you hear?
don't-cha tell anyone my sister lives
off've Central!

one day as I sat
in a diner,
I observed through the window

in broad daylight
on a sidewalk
off've Central

three men huddled together
their arms bound around each others' shoulders
heads bowed in prayer

and when the *camaradas* back home ask

¿qué hay de bueno,
qué se mira pa Alburqué?

before you can respond
they look at you, smile
and answer themselves

¿de todo, no?
   ¡en la Central!

A Poem in G Minor

back then I never realized the discipline it took
the sacrifices you made
the aloneness you endured
at just sixteen years old, what it meant to pursue your craft
while the neighborhood boys thought it crazy, funny
your nightly walks up through the twisting orchard path

sitting for hours
in a room across the wall from the chicken coop
with a henpecked sheet of music before you,
under a bare hanging light bulb's soft yellow glow
and the occasional chick, and I mean chick,
nuzzled in a box next to the electric heater's
humming and buzzing

your winter's breath
hanging in midair like an extended note
as you rubbed your hands or tucked them
under your armpits for warmth
and looking much like a chicken, I should say

would this not have made a great scene
for an Andrew Wyeth or Norman Rockwell painting?
what could it have been titled,
        "young virtuoso practicing in the hen house
          while friend looks on"?

the cobwebbed ceiling, the earthen walls, cracked, flaking
enveloping your improvised orchestrations of solitude
the scent of adobe, straw, feathers,
one foot arched and steady, the other tapping time,
winter mud on the soles of your shoes,
pausing to drain the spit from your mouthpiece across the hay strewn floor
your mumbled wisecracks about
sophisticatedly dressed men in symphonies spitting out
in similar fashion

I thought about it today
all these years later
as the afternoon's free-form radio program played Schumann
and carried poetry across the airwaves

I thought about you, me
my pockets secretly stuffed with poems
I would dare not share with anyone
because back then, in that neighborhood,
cool dudes didn't write poetry
or play the French horn

La feria y la lana

My friend Joe is describing what he calls *the prevailing forces at Wal-Mart*. "*Como dijo* Spencer, Time, Force, Space, Mass, and Energy are the five elements that keep the universe rocking 'n' rolling." "*¿Quién es* Spencer?" I ask. "Spencer *era este vato, un* mathematician, theologian, that type of *vato*." Joe makes reference to some other guy whose name he can't recall, but he says that the guy was a friend of Charlie Parker's. "*El vato era camarada* de Charlie Parker."

We're in the Garden Area relishing the tranquil environment and pleased that we are allowed to sit, undisturbed, on the patio rocking chairs. We're broke, but this afternoon the Super Center is like a free pass to an amusement park. Joe remarks that not even Donald Trump can afford himself the leisure of going to Wal-Mart, sitting in the Garden-Area, talking, casting observations and commentary, laughing and joking while the workers ignore the situation as if that is what the garden furniture is meant for.

"Donald Trump can't do this because he's too busy watching his ass, making sure he doesn't lose his money," says Joe. "Us, we can just come here and sit in these chairs for a while." We are blanketed with the scent of potting soil, plants, and flowers. Above us, a green mesh screen spanning the entire length and width of the Tool and Garden area, a thin veil between us and January's gray sky. We are daunted by all the different merchandise throughout the store, aisle and aisle, on and on. The enormity of material consumption is startling—water-proof matches, pocket railroad watches, bicycles with shock absorbers, bras, thongs, bug-eyed fish in aquariums.

"It's all here. The only thing missing," says Joe, "is the money." *"De todo hay aquí, nomás la feria hace falta."* Recalling what *un viejo vaquetón* once told me outside at Chencho's parking lot in Chamita, I reach into my pocket and pull out a pinch of lint.

> *"Hoy en día la plebe no quiere cuidar borregas.*
> *Quieren nomás la lana."*

and me

it is the 16th night
of november thirteen minutes
til midnight
the ceiling fan spins slowly
counterclockwise
above the coffee maker's drip-drop
backroom conversation spills
into the room with gossip
of bench warrants, unemployed boyfriends
and sick babies at home
teenage energy walks in
wearing leather and rustled hair
numbed face and ghostly-eyed
stirring cream under the smokey
cigarette swirl
I'll have a powder
I'll have a blueberry
giggle giggle carefree
as the doorbell tinkle
handcupped, headcapped customer

wearing "union team cuisine" logo
huffing breath into unthawed indecision
and me just sitting
with my pen ableeding
for the critics who'll come
two in one
peeling back the scabs
of another somber offering
done in observance of
the warm-cheek and content
legs crossed and yawning
their lives to scan the muted page
under the pale bed lamp glow
and me to ponder
the twisted hat madman
with crumbs on his whiskered chin
growling the world's insanity
poured black and sweetened
over the long haul
of a frosted moon

High School English

I

not long after my high school English teacher
had handed out the colored pencils
I summoned her attention

I can't see what I'm writing, Mrs. Rhutasel!
I called out
she laughed
I knew you'd pick the white one
she said

she had come to know me by then
through my daily journal entries
and unending stream of poetry and essay submissions
my passion for writing, my disdain for authority
my clumsiness with conformity

she, my first audience, harshest critic, and first truly devoted fan

I was the quiet, quiet, introverted skinny kid
with way past the shoulder length hair
and a Levi jacket on my back through every season
inside myself, I looked liked bearded Whitman
but probably more realistically resembled my *tío* Eliseo thumbing,
in kerosene lantern light, through the *Farmer's Almanac*
his green plastic billed reading cap
at a forty-five degree angle to the page

it was a love-hate relationship, me and Mrs. Rhutasel
I linguistically steering myself through the muted storm between us
communicating through punctuation marks and grammatical rules
flecked like little black sugar ants charting out across the page
and her *I like that, good job!* exclamated notations
steering me along

one day I'm just gonna write a book
without commas or periods or question marks!
I told her
well, that's fine!
she told me
but, don't leave them out on account
that you don't know where they belong!

II

in my dormitory room I read Rimbaud, Steinbeck, and Camus
I stared out through the window at the leafless trees
and sky the color of faraway from home lonesomeness
I listened to music, studied songs and lyrics
Dylan's *Greatest Hits Vol. I*
Johnny Cash Live at Folsom Prison
Al Hurricane, Los Purple Haze, Freddie Brown
and a two-album Vanguard collection of Mississippi
Delta Blues

my scratched albums turning
with a quarter cent piece
set on the stereo's needle arm
to keep the music from skipping
as one week, one season, one year
one adolescent tragedy
spun into another

and when the weather warmed
I walked the railroad tracks
and I laid out my jacket and my longing and my desperation
and I waited on the westbound trains I never hopped,
an aching for my recently deceased father
roaring through me like the rattley-clackitty-whistling
Atchison and Topeka

it was springtime and back home
one brother was cleaning out the ditches
and the other one was looking for the pruning shears, I was
sure

after walking the rails
I headed back toward campus
with an overly fondled copy
of *Bound for Glory* in my back pocket
hoping to catch a quick game of pick-up ball before dinner
and a long, cool glimpse of that one girl
what was her name?

oh, I can still smell the sweet grass
and hear the sprinklers going strong
something 'bout her in a tight red T-shirt
in that time long ago now gone

III

I liked girls that had good penmanship
and could exercise the rules of proper grammar correctly
knowing where to put the comma and the period
and the semicolon meant something
I don't know what, but I had an attraction to it
it may have come from a time back in fourth grade
when I had beat the prettiest and smartest girl

in a spelling bee contest
that year I had risen out of the ranks of the "D-group" students
the ones bound for prison and/or a life lived
and terminated before the age of thirty
the ones who spoke the Spanish of their grandparents
as a first language
with accents thick and soft and musky
as the upturned earth rolling off
their grandfathers' horse drawn plows

the ones who found themselves having to make
accommodations
in their inherited world perspective for Biff and Tiff
and the prospect of a janitorial job or a starched mechanic's shirt
with their real baptismal-given-name scrawled across
their lapel in cursive writing

and I can still smell the waxy fat orange crayon
melting on a sunlit desktop
while I stood in the corner where they sent little boys
who wanted to draw cars instead of turkeys and pumpkins,
the rest of the class behind me
slumping over their assignments
like neat rows of punctuation marks

and I knew what an apostrophe was and how to use it
without ever having been told
though I refrained from using it
since I knew that knowing more
than you were supposed to know
meant that your silence couldn't be trusted
and *sa-na-magón-sito* you'd better darn well know it!

IV

In junior high, *el culón* Fatso
the music appreciation teacher
flung up his orchestrating arms one more and a half final time
and marched off to the admin office to charm the secretaries
and sip on soft drinks while we sat stewing in the overheated
metal annex building coauthoring pages of "I shall not hit anyone"
for the bullies who'd hit you again
if you didn't write your share
of their 900 lines

but, that was before boarding school and Mrs. Rhutasel

V

In boarding school
the first thing they said to me
was the last thing they said to me
which was *if you don't cut your hair, you can't come to school here*

Maria, the school's ESL teacher, counselor, and friend of Mrs. Rhutasel
heard from someone that I was an artist and wrote poetry
she'd heard from someone that my father had recently died

I, being fluent in Spanish, proclaimed that I had no need
for bilingual classes and my strong self-determination
and inner anti-wimpiness mocked the need for counselors

but, Maria called me out of the hall one day
befriended me and lip-pointed me toward
a blank wall crying out for a mural

ahi está, she said, *pinta lo que quieras*

and then she reached into her desk drawer
and handed me my first collection of literature
       Literatura Chicana: Texto y contexto

toma, she said, *something I think you'll like*

VI

"El Louie" and "Un Trip Through the Mind Jail"

¡a la máquina, a la fregada, a la mustard!

my literary senses were startled awake
by the language and themes
that these two poems were revealing to me

the colloquial poetics of a poetic voice
sounding like mine
written in that distinct dialectical syntax
of those dudes hanging out
behind the school gym

remember the flunked out older guys
sitting in the seats behind you
slingshotting their index finger
at the back of your skull?

it was a voice like that!

hey, before then
I didn't know
I could write
sound and make
the language of the page
seem like it was coming
from the tongue of my
deepest personal introverted
most unpunctuated
pero bien locote
self!

Homenaje a raul r. salinas,
maestro, poeta, y camarada

II.

¡Traigan sus palas, plebe!

Ya las campanas están doblando,

'horita vamos al chilito

as I was saying, Nancy

you who ask questions and whose interest
so compels me to engage in conversations
marred by all too-quick, break-over,
gotta get back to work interruptions
    while I walk away
        still fumbling for lucid explanations
           for whatever it was
                that we were almost talking about

and all becomes lost anecdote
    life's story line unfinished
        and, no, in my family we are not that smart

but, how nice of you to see, I mean, say that
because maybe we were
and at times it has, did
feel that way

but, now we are incomplete again

mi familia
my family

twenty years ago my father died
and that many years it took to get to the letting go
and then
the death of my brother last summer

again death again

and over the years
another brother gone down
the down road of
otro día, otra pena

again life again

although at one time it was not as such

the irrigation ditch in front of my mother's house gurgled
with the sound of water snaking under the swaying tree
through lazy dog-eyed summer afternoons that hummed
with the sleepy lullaby of so much to do

aah, I'll get to it tomorrow

and while one generation slooowly nodded off
another one was waking up to life's harsh questions
for which there were no real questions
for the answers that became seemingly more unreal
and undeserving than the questions themselves

          life, Nancy
was a little all too eloquent
for the language we bared through calamities and tragedies
and phones ringing in the startled night
leaving us numb with stubborn look-ahead gazes
and our tongues in a knot

and yet
       there are also memories of Sunday afternoons
          special
             because
                just because
and celebrated with great taco dinners
and my sister's homemade salsa
spicy and juicy
dripping down chins
and laughter splattering through
the kitchen's north window
across the orchard and

away
>
away
>
>
away

and a baby that came unplanned with new life and joy
savior of almost broken-beyond-repair
spirit home refrain, laughing
>
again
>
>
again
>
>
>
again

and now she too is grown

her high school commencement this past spring
marks a new turn in the road
and we make way without realizing that we do

and when she sang
"don't ever lose the light in your eyes"
to a standing ovation
I stepped outside and the tears burned
against the wind in my eyes
and I walked across the meadow
and I stood under a grove of aspen trees
their trunks carved and etched with names and initials
of who loved who
and when
and from then until always

and I thought of my brother
and how I missed him so
and how I wished he'd been there

and later on in the afternoon
after the reception and a slight rain
a double rainbow across the sky
informed me that he had been

    around here,
we just take the good with the bad
    my mother used to say

on Friday nights sometimes I'll get the urge
to eat Beanie Weenies and Vienna Sausages on crackers
and I think of my friend, Timmy
teenage friend, blood brother
shared dreamer of life to come

and how we'd sit
parked across La Otra Banda bridge
in his '72 Cutlass lowrider
through predawn picnics
laughing and eating pork 'n' beans and weenies
and sharing a last swig of Boone's Farm
with the rushing spring thaw
rolling under and rumbling
       away
         away
           away

it is a senseless place

all this
it does not make sense
to me

I was reprimanded
at six years old

elementary school
my drawing and my
who I was

taken away from me

so now

tonight
this morning
on an afternoon
never before

like now and this

I am asked
to reveal

the light grown out

of that darkness

where I stood

punished in the corner
of my classroom

nose against the wall

I

heard behind me
pages of Dick and Jane
turn over

I could read as well as the best reader
but I learned how to read
something else

silence became
my language

I found strength
in weakness

I found expression

in thoughts without
voice

twenty-nine years later

same teachers applaud

my recitals
and the book
I bring to them

to my village

this senseless place

throughout the years

I have let the cobwebs
in corners gather

I

know the

silence

of the spider

and the language that weaves

I heard then

I hear now

the pages turning

Entre preguntas y respuestas

andando de visita por el barrio de los malditos
en una mañana de primavera con el sol ya brillando fuerte
me topé con un paisano en el parqueadero de la estafeta

le pregunté, ¿es verdad, he oído decir que en tus tiempos
te avientavas pa cantar?

y él mi respondió

> *¡cantabas, grillo cabrón!*

y en decir eso
levantó la pata
y zapatió la tierra

> *no, ya se acabó la parrandota, cuate*

y en su distinguida manera
de responder sus propias inquiridas
adelantó la plática

> *¿qué andas haciendo, vesitando?*
> *¿cómo está la familia, bien?*
> *¿dónde estás viviendo, Alburqué?*

y por hay nos fuimos
hasta que las sombritas echadas bajo los pinos se movieron
anunciando que ya era tiempo de seguirle al camino

> *¿bueno, pa dónde vas 'hora, fishin'?*
> *¿pa dónde, Tres Ritos?*
> *¿estará picando? izque con lombriz*

Como una extinción de verdad floriando

the apricot clippings in the vase
on the table have begun to blossom

today a young girl in the writing class
presented me with her assignment
she would like to know if it is a poem

if I tell her it is
would I be lying?
if I tell her it isn't
would I be telling her the truth?

the apricot branch will eventually bud
small protrusions of leaves will begin to appear
making the inside air thick with flower
the beeless silence buzzing
a long season awaiting cut short

the student has titled her poem
"Extinción de mi identidad"

her first lines read like this
¿quién eres,
dónde estás,
por qué tú quieres ser tú?

!tú no eres tú mismo¡

as a child I loved summers
little green apples, fuzzy apricots
I liked plucking their soft pit and squeezing it

with my pockets stuffed full of green fruit
I ran through neighboring orchards
followed paths that led down to the swimming hole
learned how to dog paddle and how to skip stones

her poem continues
>   *decepción, deshonestidad, rumores*
>   *dejan un agujero en nuestra identidad*
>   *una plaga en nuestra alma*

summers come
but no time is made to dam up the stream
weave a net of logs and boulders
no time made to sit and wade
waiting for the trout to dart out from under the bank
these are summers when a good pair of sneakers
will not be ruined by tadpole expeditions, murky water,
sticks and stones

>   *espera los enamores*
>   *entristeciendo*

she writes

I pause, contemplating
the possible meaning
of her two-line stanza
I swirl the words around my tongue
the vowel sounds, the syllables
a tart pronunciation ripening towards sweetness lingers

>   *espera los enamores*
>   *entristeciendo*

her lines, each verse scribbled
in the ink off a bad pen
just above the faded line

>   *permita que controle*
>   *nuestra vida*
>   *¡yo soy quien soy!*

it is past midnight now
my daughters, my wife asleep
I couldn't, so I got up to read
found myself staring at the flowering apricot

>   if one of my daughters should ask
>   whether the apricot branch is alive or not
>   and how is it so

>   if I tell her it is
>   would I be lying?
>   if I tell her it isn't
>   would I be telling her the truth?

>   whose hand in this household
>   will determine the branch's fate
>   next week, or the next?
>   its withered leaves on brittle stems
>   the blossoms yellowed and flaked across the table
>   the water gone stale

>   *¿por qué te preocupas?*
>   *¡regrésame mi identidad!*

her final lines

Simple Math

I don't know what today will bring tomorrow
what it will allow, what it will disallow

what it may add or subtract
what will be canceled out

it is a process of trial by error
and I'm known to leave a path
like eraser grains on paper

my life

my life with you
my life without you

vows formed into flesh
and two become one
an abstraction rising from a definitive then
toward an infinitive beyond

is there a way to calculate
what is meant
the actual meaning realized

of a life with
of a life without?

last night I said to our niece
that a person who is good at math
already has one thing that it takes to be successful

I'm not sure she understood what I meant

but, my father used to say that the world with-
out math is like a hamburger
without the meat

and I think I know what he meant

I who have always had difficulty
comprehending how one and one make one

my life with
my life without
you

Los caminantes

homenaje a primo Bill

no sabemos acual de nosotros le tocará primero
pero es cierto, uno caminará antes que el otro

por eso será entonces que nos la pasamos
como luego dices
buscándole carne al chicharrón

aquí sentados esta tarde bajo de un sombraje
con las orejas y lenguas apuntiaditas y estiradas
como la navajita del santero
relumbrando vuelta con los rayos del sol

nos tocó ver un año más, un año menos

ya de febrero pa delante los perros buscan sombra
decía aquel primo que ya también se nos fue

en otra conversación reciente tomé nota
en lo que me decía un amigo
reflejando en haber perdido a su papá

en ese día, hermano, se me acabó la sombra
del árbol donde yo sombreaba

y yo también que llegué a pasar por ese luto
de aquella nube cuelgando como manto
lloviznando por el valle de lágrimas de mi juventud

en algún otro tiempo
pueda que San Francisco nos acompañaría
en estas pláticas de contemplación
y él también se pondriá a dibujar crucitas en la tierra
con una jarra de costal

¿qué te parece, Francisco? le preguntaríanos
¿qué dicho nos quieres contar?

no es a la muerte que le temo, pero a la cruzada
¿qué no fueron esas las palabras que el lector habló
para el entierro de aquel paisano?

y yo, al oírlas, desde esa chica edad
las recogí del viento que las soplaba
como cizañas bailando todo el caminito
desde la iglesia hasta el camposanto

se miran más alegres los camposantos
que la plaza vieja
comentó en ese día un reflejor

fijándose que en esa vecindad
las bendiciones se les dan a los vivos
y las flores a los difuntos

andando entre las sepulturas
se dobló la cachucha, diciendo

quizás están muy contentos allá en la gloria
porque no llaman ni escriben

y parado sobre el sepulcro
su imagen destendida sobre la tierra, apiladita
fresca, negra y sudada, reclamó

¡traigan sus palas, plebe!

ya las campanas están doblando
'horita vamos al chilito

Most Skin Hit Road

the visiting community activist contingency
comes into her home as invited guests
politely invading her life with
gift baskets of hugs, laughter, and
you're looking great! salutations

their warm blessings filling the room
with wide-open arm offerings of good conversation
and quick-comeback humorous anecdotes
to transport her past nagging thoughts

of next month's mortgage
the leaking faucets
the molding wallboard
the house too big
left over from a bad divorce

leaving her with the two children
to carry on with the domesticities
of this place stayed at too long
longer than what was planned
longer than what was wished for
longer than what *until I'm done with school* might've meant

what would make a man
pick up his life
his personal possessions
what he deems as his most precious belongings
and leave his small children

his name and the shape of their eyes
the blood that runs through their veins
their tender skin, their soft complexion
the color of his own mother's
the resonance of his grandfather's laughter
and musical quality in their voice and pronunciations

more than mere traces of himself
upon their temperament, the slow or fast to decision
the methodical calculation
his impulsive nature and neurotic tendency
for quick resolution

these being his traits
stepping back to check the doorknob
in his final leaving
his girlfriend awaiting his arrival
two states away with tomorrow night's
dinner reservations

we stand in the kitchen
fondling for conversation and dialogue
dipping for some topic interesting enough
to make ourselves appear intelligent, compassionate
and genuinely concerned about world issues
and the plight of all humankind
la frontera, las desaparecidas, los braceros, las maliquidoras
that war, this war, that president, *that president!*

she, an attractive woman, still young
speaking fluently in two languages
her eyes dark and warm as the border sundown
photos taken at different stages of motherhood
on the refrigerator door
the magnet poetry scattered and nonsensical
"most skin hit road"

outside the humidity is heavy as a street blanket
shards of broken glass
on the front porch steps
Juárez's flickering lights in the distance
El Paso trains whistling by
her memories of Laredo

my attention nailed now
to the broken rosary necklace
hanging from a porch column

our own histories
who we are
where we come from

could be reinvented
in the next sentence uttered
the next clever line spoken
the next interjection of humor and
sincere display of pleasantries
masking over the face of a new persona

any further answers to all possible questions
made more believable
than the reality of our own true selves
our own leaking faucets, ragged lawns
oil stained driveways, two nights of dinner dishes
and yesterday morning's half filled cereal bowls
on the counter

who has time for the trivial things
when we spend our clichéd lives
adorned with momentary lapses of reason
and an existence busied
by just trying to make tattered ends meet

In the Words of My Students

my writer's self
was just buried under
  at some point in the midst
      of this grief

  among headstones

  a life full of children
  full of marriage

      hypnogenic

i like the idea of
    hmm. . . .
        well, i wanna be

coming to words

remaining in silence
  to hear
      the chaos

it means nothing
  other than that

and
  hmm . . . well
      so many things
      so many things
      so many things

          ocean time

vast like ocean time

and i have a rebellion
against
    result
      although
        i'm really
          into
            scissors

like Marcia's husband
    my marriage
      died

how did you get to poetry?

        i started humming a song
        from 1962
        ain't it funny how

        the night moves

        when you just don't seem
        to have as much to lose

        and here i am
        with autumn closing in

and so there i was
    at one foot above sea level
    and i just started
writing

i was gonna be

but it never panned out

i wasn't scientific enough
    earrings and such

unto ashes
                the curtain society
                morsyphillicita
                la gonorrhea

i don't even know what
a pagan is anymore

which is whatever

open mic night
    at some bar
        in Salem

energenic

and, well, i could write about
this cup
or something
like that

and you know
that last thing he said?

that's something i was gonna say

Consejito en el caminito

me topé con el vecino en el caminito
¿cómo les fue en la 'cequia? le pregunte

no, ya hoy en día no hay peones, me dijo
ni pendejos, hacen más con el disability

luego no quieren trabajar,
y no les puede uno decir nada

hoy en día es mejor ser gallina que gallo

Moments and Seasons

she walks in
asks for a cup of coffee
no cream, no sugar, she says
and one plain donut

she pulls out a small pouch of coins
drops it on the counter
thirty cents, okay?

she's a white girl
flaca, pale faced and freckled
do i seem in a bad mood? she asks
the question is addressed to no one in
particular
ah, no, not really, the male attendant
replies

are you? i ask
hmm, sort of, she says
so, it could go either way? I ask
yeah, she says
marching away with her coffee
leaving behind a powdered veil
of menthol smoke

warm spring weather came early last
month
but it's been cold again lately

a season, a day
a moment in transition

it could go either way

Unemployment Lines

at the unemployment office
I know it can be a two hour deathly wait
before one's name is called out
so I find a chair and bury my head
in a book that I brought to read

sitting beside me, a man and a woman converse
talk of years past, of people they knew

> *and Leonard, is he still in prison?*
> *yeah, he's still doing time*
> *well, that's good, I guess, means he's still alive*

a young girl walks in, short black halter top
and airbrushed-on jeans
her breasts pouting up past a too low neckline
the men, the women, all stare
whether they'd like to or not

Leonard's friends exchange stories
> *yeah, my ex, she just wants my money*
> *I tell her, well, go work then!*

and they laugh between the irony
life, huh, she tells him, *it's crazy, the things we get into,*
he agrees
the rest of us caught silently in their exchange agree, as well

his arms are thick with hair
and tattoos of skulls

and scrawled out
indecipherable letters of the alphabet

> *yeah, this chick that was riding with me once,* he tells her
> *got her jacket belt caught on my wheel*
> *I didn't even know it until I got to the next light*
> *I went back, she was alright, just fell off, didn't get hurt or nothing*
> *she was pissed though*

"just fell off, didn't get hurt," what does he mean?
this story just drops off, I want to know a little more, a lot more
I mean, how fast was the bike going when she fell off
did she ruin the belt, scrape her nose,
did they drink a lot of beer afterwards?

and so the time drags by, the line lengthens
now and then people unbury their heads
from their midmorning dragging into noon thoughts
women adjust their bra straps
scold their kids with unfulfilled warnings
the folks behind the counter look at us
holding their half empty cups of coffee

ah, if only there was a dollar for every story

You, Our Rain

the recent rains
may make it seem to the tourists
that it has been a season
of good weather
one in keeping with
the demands of this region

the sound of thunder in the far off
afternoon
the formation of clouds
cupped and nudged in the gentle curve
of the nearby far away
like a child lulled sweetly through

but, it has been a hot, dry and burning summer

winter did not come as it was wished for
and spring must've wished upon itself
that which we did not want
but these last few weeks of afternoon rain
have replenished us to a point of comfort
where our greetings of *good day*
or *good afternoon*

mean just that

and that, in a time of harshness,
is more than good enough

along the walking trail
of the west rim
the shadows of our noses
fall into coyote paw prints etched
into the damp soil

instinctively we sniff the winds
trying to catch a scent
of something to alert us back
to our primordial selves

it is agreed

the scent of sage is not as pungent as usual
and the moisture clings like a wet serape to the ground
where we walk across an area of vast pools of water
formed of recent rain

the tadpoles are fat
and plentiful
like Botticelli nymphs
playful in the murkiness

it is agreed

it is rather late in the season
for tadpoles
but they like us have been waiting on the rains

the persistent breeze
the piñon scrub
juniper
chamizo pardo

a taut thread of web
strung across the trail,
a week off from work to write
to be with other writers

who is deserving of all of this
on a midafternoon work week?

not I

but you
you, back home
with the children
your laughter and the singing of your voice
you, our afternoon rain

you are the storm cloud that delivers
what it promises
in times of dry
the self-served small portion
so that someone else may have

you, the strong
ripple
the replenishing sprinkle
the oncoming plentiful

set as the stones of summer,
affirmed in your position
the big black boulder
smoothed and carved
jagged and knotted

we will survive

you, our rain

the drought of my selfishness

III.

No matter how much things change,

that which gave us life, sustained us,

will always be with us,

here, aquí—en el pecho,

en el corazón

Lowcura

An Introspective *Virtual Cruise*

Through an American Subcultural Tradition

". . . nostalgia gleams with the dull brilliance
of a chrome airplane on the rusted hood
of a '56 Chevy

. . . daydreams of walking barefoot
on the soft grass
down by the river
where dragonflies buzzed all day
have now decayed
like the fallen cottonwoods
along the gnarled paths
of the Río Embudo

where free-form poetry
mixed with cheap beer
on warm nights by the riverbanks

and stories of lowered '49 Fleetlines
with flamejobs and spinners
were cast into the dark wind . . ."

Hearts and Arrows

Years Later, I Would Hear Stories

I remember it this way, Magdalena. As a small child I would accompany my grandmother on her walks to and from my mother's house, which was about a mile and a half away. We would follow a walking path along the Río Embudo, a small stream weaving along the northern edge of the village where I grew up. There was a certain place along this walk that we always looked forward to. It was there, just off the sand and gravel trail under the shade of the towering cottonwoods and heavy scent of river willow and summer heat, where we would stop for a short respite. It was at this section along the river where some of the villagers' discarded automobiles sat in abandonment, a sort of village car cemetery. One car in particular attracted our attention, a faded pink 1949 Chevrolet Fleetline flipped over on its back and succumbing to the rust and ruin of cars that meet such a fate. Grandma would walk over to it, and we would stand there momentarily, our hands caressing the fat-fendered Chevy. *"Este era el carro del Levi,"* she would say, pointing to her grandson's car. We would silently pay our respects and move on. Years later, I would hear stories about my cousin Levi and his lowered Fleetline and learn that he had been one of the first lowriders in northern New Mexico; the region around Española that in time became regarded affectionately as the "Lowrider Capital of the World."

Resuello y Alma

I began cruising when I was about twelve years old with some older cousins who would take me along on their nightly cruises into town. It was in the early 1970s and the beginning stages of lowriding in Española. The factions between the hot rodders and the lowriders were visibly displayed under the streetlight glow of shopping center parking lots and along main street. My cousin, lil' Joe, recently moved back from California, had brought his passion for lowriding with him and transplanted it into the quickly forming popular pastime. Lil' Joe would pass on down to me my first lowrider, a copper brown 1959 Chevrolet station wagon with velvet curtains, shag carpeting and a donut steering wheel. Truthfully, I never replaced the dead battery in the car and was never able to take it out on the cruise. Nonetheless, I'd accompany my cousins into Espa', usually cruising with my cousin Raymond in his dropped 1955 Chevy pickup truck. It was a beautiful piece of nostalgia painted a Diamond Black, rolling on baby-moon chromed rims on gangster-wide whitewall tires, with hood mounted dummy spotlights and Bob Dylan on his stereo.

And so, Magdalena, there begins my story—my earliest recollections of lowriders and some of my first experiences and observations from within the breath and soul, *resuello y alma*, of a distinct American subcultural tradition, lowriding.

Eran en los Dias de los Heroes

The lowrider has always been a representation of individual expression and identity, with connotations of a rebellious and nonconforming nature. The *vato loco* archetype became the model for the lowrider, and it was that paragon of social deviance that formed the alluring quality that sometimes attracted a young Chicano feeling the need to affirm his individuality and social status. In my contemplations regarding the lowrider lifestyle, as I have witnessed it and lived it, as I have loved it and have attempted to outgrow my attraction to it, with no success, I have come to recognize that the lowrider bore not only the burden of his own individual identification, but also sustained the cultural traditions of language, religion, spirituality, and allegiance to community, proclaiming proudly, even arrogantly, his existence in the reality of a social status smirked at by the status quo. I can recall as a young boy seeing these individuals parked in their lowered rides under the shade down by the river, or along roadside turnarounds, or cruising slowly through some dirt road weaving through the village, their slow rides bouncing rhythmically to the grooves spilling out from their car radios.

Los Heroes

los watchávamos
cuando   pasaban
echando jumito azul
en sus ranflas aplanadas
como ranas de ojelata

eran en los días
de los heroes

cuando había heroes
turriqueando en
lengua mocha
y riza torcida

Q-volé

ahora nomás   pasan
los recuerdos
uno tras del otro
y mi corazón
baila

bendición

bendición es
estar contento

Señor, gracias por . . .

gracias por todo

Por Vida

For any lowrider, his car may be the ultimate form of expression and representation of how he views himself and wants to be seen, but the story would be incomplete if one were to showcase the lowrider only through the marvelous and beautiful creation of the customized car. I believe, Magdalena, that the last thing in poetry is the poem, as I also believe that the last thing in lowriding is a lowered ride. The defining essence of what makes someone a lowrider is something that cannot be relegated down to a material possession. In many instances, individuals who did not own a car or have a driver's license or the means to earn the wages that enabled them to possess and maintain a cool ride were those who best upheld the ideal image of what it was to be a *low rider*—a social misfit understood neither within his own culture nor within the Western Anglo-Saxon world to which he could not relate. For that type of individual, there was no way out. His *locura* was with him from the beginning to the end. *Por vida.* For those who didn't and for those who did persevere, who did not buy in or sell out, *sangre joven y veteranos igual que no dejaron cae la bandera*, who lived through *la vida loca* and came out laughing, grabbing at life's sweet hustle, for the honor and glory of not caring to know any other way, it is in their own *locura* and from their own perspective that the lowrider story should also be told.

En tu memoria

el Leonard
no le caiva que lo llamaran Lenny
sandy blonde raspy voice
green eyes toward the distant
crazy
walking out of the Allsup's in Mora
unbuttoned shirt and a quart of vodka

stuffed in his jeans
  ¡watcha lo que traigo aquí!
he said, as we drove away
  ¡qué jodido, huero!
¿qué no tienes miedo que te
    tuersan?
he chuckled, popped the bottle open
  ¡ponle! he said
¡ay, qué Lenny!
    nomás los recuerdos quedan
aquí te va
    un buen pajuelazo en tu memoria

Theirs is an endearing language of colloquialisms, pachuquisms, regional dialects and a car culture vocabulary as colorful as a trunk-hood mural and as vibrant as the memories they've painted and etched across our own everyday palettes of blandness and conformity.

El Chapulín y El Bionic

me topé con el Chapulín y el Bionic
en un Swap-Meet en Alburqué

pura ojelata vieja, tu sabes
y hay se comenzó el tripe

how much did you say?

Fifty

I'll take that one and one of these
and two of those
yeah, one and one of these
one of those and how much for one of these?
okay do I get one of those for free
you know, as a bonus for two of those
one of these and one of those?

well, that'll be seventy-eight

I thought you said forty-five?

forty-five? One of those alone is forty-five
give me seventy-five

I'll give you seventy
no, seventy-five

Bionic stands in the hot sun
wisps of hair from his ponytail
cling to his sweating forehead

¡y, wáchate este, qué locote!
¿qué tanto? *Ten.* Ten? *Ten*
bueno, save it for me

that's a head lamp ring from a '37, no? *Yup*

Cool! ahi vengo por el later

How Can I Tell You, Baby?

Well, Magdalena, I hope your interest hasn't begun to wane by now. This whole lowrider thing, it's actually a multilayered phenomenon. How can one begin to describe or explain something that is so big and so small, so deep and so shallow, so high and so low, that it practically defies formal definition? I mean, could a definition such as this suffice?

Lowrider (ló′ri′dah) 1. A car culture lifestyle with its origins in California. 2. An individual whose personal identity is manifested through his automobile. 3. A car, truck, or bicycle that has been modified to achieve a lowered profile.

And even if a definitive description could be applied to illustrate the aesthetic qualities and physical characteristics of the lowrider, there are still other insights that can be presented with underlying social, cultural, and psychological parallels. It's been proclaimed that New Mexico's cultural landscape has changed more dramatically within the last 30 years than in the previous 400. For the lowrider *del norte de Nuevo México*, whose daily life revolved around a direct ancestral lineage and tradition linked to *la santa fe, madre, familia, tierra y agua, cosas nuestras y sagradas*, a nurturing unconscious manifestation of spiritual sustenance formed a shield against the eminent winds of change and strengthened that inherent will of perseverance. Social commentaries and observations, equally humorous and ironic in their perspective, were interwoven into the riff-raffing, bullshittin', teasing dialogues and oral story reverberations *de platica y carrilla*.

Wheels

how can I tell you
baby, oh honey, you'll
never know the ride
the ride of a lowered Chevy
slithering through the
blue dotted night along
Riverside Drive Española

poetry rides the wings
of a '59 Impala
yes, it does
and it points
chrome antennae towards

'Burque stations rocking
oldies Van Morrison
brown eyed girls
Creedence and a
bad moon rising
over Chimayo

and I guess
it also rides
on muddy Subarus
tuned into new age radio
on the frigid road
to Taos on weekend
ski trips

yes, baby
you and I are two
kinds of wheels
on the same road

listen, listen
to the lonesome humming
of the tracks we leave
behind

Wonderin' Where I Went Wrong Going Right

And how descriptive or accurate could a portrayal of the lowrider be
without exemplifying the linguistic orations of a slow-riding, time-
stealing story? Are you still with me, Magdalena, *¿Tiraremos otra
vuelta? Bueno*, sit back, turn up the jams and enjoy the ride.

Easynights and a Pack of *Frajos*

Rosendo used to ride the buses
scoring phone numbers from *rucas*
he met at the *parque* or
along Central's bus stops and diners

three to five numbers a day, homes!
he'd say, *by the end of the week
I know I'll get lucky with
at least one, 'ey*

*maybe she'll have her own canton
and I'll drop by with a bottle of wine
and some good smoke
¡y vamonos recio, carnal!*

and he'd laugh, tilting his head back
taking a long drag from a Camel regular
and then he'd look at me
and laugh again, saying
¡iii, este vato!
sometimes, I just don't know
about you, bro

one night I was down at Jack's shooting pool
when the bartender yelled out
that there was a phone call
for someone whose name sounded like mine
and I was real surprised
that it was for me, you know

well, it was this fine babe from the Westside
that I'd met a few weeks before
she said that my roommate
had told her I'd be there
she said she'd been wondering
what I'd been doing
and how come I hadn't called
she wanted me to go over
I said, *great! I want to shoot a few more*
games of pool, but I'll be there in a while.

not that I was really interested
in pool anymore
but, hey I couldn't let on
like I didn't ever get
those kinda calls, you know

not like those *vatos* down at Tito's
with tattoos and dead-aim stares did
leaning back against the wall
flirting with some *ruca* over the phone
laughing and teasing while the jukebox
plays Sam Cooke and me sitting there
watching and wondering where I
went wrong going right

I asked her if there was anything
she wanted me to bring over
some wine, maybe
and she said, *yeah*
that sounds good!
and could you bring some cigarettes too?

so there I was, going down the street
being all *truchas* for the *jura*
'cause I didn't want nothin'
to ruin this *movida*, you know

well, I pulled into the Casa Grande
and asked for a bottle of Easynights
and a pack of *frajos*
and I sat looking through the drive-up window
at the naked pinup girls on the wall

and I started thinking of home, so far away
and how oftentimes I had nowhere to go
wishing I knew some nice girl
I could drop by to visit
and watch a *mono* with
or just to sit and talk to

it was a rainy night
a beautiful rainy night
and the streets were all black and wet
neon lights reflecting off of everything
and running down the street
in streams of color

and I thought of Rosendo
and how he was going to laugh
and I knew he was going to want
to know everything
¿órale, serio?
chale, you're jiving, homes

¡no, serio
her name's Carmela!

¿serio, homes?

yeah!

¿no?

¡yeah, deveras!

¡iii, este vato!
then I saw myself in the mirror
and I started laughing

sometimes, I just don't know
about you, bro

And no matter how many the years, how far removed, or how long the distance from the road once traveled, what it is still is, because it was, because we were, because we still are, at heart, cruisers cruising through the homeland. So no matter how much things change, that which gave us life, sustained us, will always be with us, here, *aquí, en el pecho, en el corazón!*

One Last Cruise:
Taos Plaza

    this morning I decided
    to throw one more cruise
    through the plaza

    en memoria de primo Bill
    y de los resolaneros de aquellos tiempos

    those men who had found their circle
    come together
    in the presence of
    each other

        like everything else around here
        it seems all is become memory

    some Saturday mornings
    my father would make the twenty mile trip
    into town

    we'd park at the Cantú Furniture
    parking lot that sits atop
    the old 7-11 building
    off Paseo del Pueblo Sur

it was exciting for me then
as a small boy
to know that our car
was moving across the roof
of the store below

and now, I still find it amusing,
how did that sort of engineering feat
arrive in Taos?

the other evening
I pulled into that same parking lot
and for a brief moment
contemplated leaving my truck there,
but for the sign that read

**Customer Parking Only
All Others Towed Away!**

this morning
as I cruised into the plaza
I saw one lone, recognizable,
living, remnant, figure
standing in faded jeans
white T-shirt, Converse canvas All Stars
and a bundle of newspapers
strapped around his shoulder

it was *el Paulie*
flattopped, square-jawed
and looking thirty years ago
still the same

but, where were you *primo Bill?*

the park benches deserted
the covered portals no longer bursting
with children clinging to their mother's shopping stride

mama's strolling elegant
black hair curled
red lipstick
the purse and coat
was it that Jackie Kennedy period
or was it Connie Francis?

I look out at the *parque*
los callejoncitos, las sombritas

> *¡nada!*
¿qué pasó con la palomía,
con los Indios envueltos en sus frezadas?

¿qué paso con la mini-falda?

I reach for the radio knob
and I crank up Santana

I let the sound of the timbales
   snap
      against
the vacant hollowness of memory
         against the plaza's deserted facade
against the songbird's mournful eulogy

I notice a group of tourists
congregating next to where the old army surplus
used to be

   I look
      don't look
         I look again

they pretend not to

I know I'm on trial

I let off the gas pedal
and cruise in slowly

I lean back
into the seat, lowdown
and make myself comfortable
controlling the steering wheel
with one finger

here's one for the ol' times, baby!

¡*dale vuelo!*

I remember cruising through the plaza
as a teenager with the Luna brothers, Pedro and Rupert

I remember Rupert
badass *Califa's loco*
coming out to spend time with his grandparents
whenever he was wanted by the law back in Madera
I remember him
leaning far back into the seat of that black '67 Chevy
sporting spit-shined *calcos* with one leg up on the dashboard
and finger-snappin' time to War tunes on the 8-track stereo

his *locura,* cocky and loud
estilo California, nothin' like *Nuevo's*
quiet and proud

back then *Taosie* wasn't a lowriding town
chale, low Impalas came from Espa'
I remember Rupert blurting out the window
to some *Taoseño* dudes staring us out
    whatcha lookin' at, ese
    we're just lowriding!

well, I remember those times
being mostly like that

the predictable unknown, lurking
waiting around like some badass dude
leaning back with one bent leg up against the wall

and somehow we'd slip through each incident
acting like it hadn't mattered whether we would or not

this morning
the people hanging out
  by the coffee shop
    laugh and languish

their carefree tourist manner void of history, of memory
neither attachment nor sentiment to time and place
no scars as enduring testaments
to the questions posed, the answers given

a young girl stretches out
against the oncoming morning
her breasts
her form
that figure

¡mmm, gringa!

what am I thinking?

I'm the writing instructor
of this summer's poetry class!

I can't think
act
look
this way
but hell,
I pull my shoulder back
turn my head
and stare

mmm, baby, baby!

at the stop light
  a young *vato*
    long hair
      and a ponytail

looks at me
  catches
    the riff

he knows the *movida*

a tight smile forms across his mouth

      Oye Cómo Va
      Mi Ritmo

      ¡bongo, boom, da!
      Mi Ritmo!
      tsssssssss_____ !!

    for you, *carnal!*

one last cruise
around
    the plaza

What Does All This All Mean?

And because you've asked me for my insights and contributions, Magdalena, I've tried. Though really, what can I offer you but this? Broken-tongue stories, some thoughts, a few poems, a low-down cruise with a panoramic view into a seemingly ominous future and a reconciliation born out of a come-what-may resiliency—*¡y que venga lo que venga!*

Maybe you can find a way to break it all up, fragment it, present it in a more presentable way, wring out the blood, harness the spirit, translate the non-translatable, remove the music from the song, raise the ride back up and still call it low. *Que te vaya bien.* I couldn't do it even if I knew how. *Es todo—un viaje por mi Lowcura, por mi Tierra Sagrada.*

New and Rejected Works

I watched a dropped
metallic lavender colored '66 LeMans
pulling out of the AutoZone onto Sunset
sporting 5/60s, Cragars, curb feelers, and rabbit ears

rabbit ears?

simón, a true period piece, *ese!*

a mid-seventies testament
a real gem of the Sunday afternoon cruise
an Ichi Coo Park, everyone's-eyes-on-it
car wash bitchin'
piece-of-ass scoring *ranfla*

what does all this all mean?

what true literary aficionado
could understand or bare even the slightest interest
in this ghost-patterned paint, chrome and rubber observation?

will this poem
be allowed to exist
alongside other genres of poetry?

to say the least of its highly improbable publication possibilities
in reputable, established "American" literary journals
that hold, in their editorial exercising power
the ability to affirm and measure
a writer's worthwhile poetic existence

no, probably not

yet, that bumper scraping cruiser
dressed in accessories from a past era
and cruising down the street literally naked
to the general public mind
was nothing but *pura poesía* to me

a statement of personal taste
much as others' interest akin to stamp collecting,
gun and knife shows or extravagant doll exhibits

as well as, say, literary journal subscriptions
for those who must have their poetic fix
mailed to them every month,
curbing an appetite for the compositional qualities
and technical structuring of a language
that works best with a certain degree of abstraction

is this poem abstract enough?

does it carry a central theme engaging a universal dialogue?
is it Eastern enough to satisfy the taste of the self-absorbent
intellectually sophisticated Western palette?

will the U.S. poet laureate nod his head in approval
and suggest that it at least be considered
placed next to the greatest poems ever written
about cats curled up on a windowsill?

hmm, maybe it's a little bit too literal
too barrio, too East LAish
or just too Aztlanish

there are, of course, some great literary enthusiasts
that could easily decipher the blue dot
'67 Cougar taillight blinking like a Christmas tree *carrucha*,
with the boogie-woogie *rolas* riffing
out've a set of organ pipes,
and a dashboard saint protecting us
from that which does not understand us,
chain steering wheel chariot
with the red lights flashing in the mirror

red lights flashing in the mirror?
maybe it's the poetry police!
¡ponte truchas, carnal!

great literary enthusiasts who can't even read
who do not have subscriptions to anything of self-interest
because nothing they were ever given to read
made sense to them either

great literary enthusiasts holed up in a lockup facility
who sit waiting for their final sentence to be read to them
who without explanation or implication are told
we are simply following due process

whose hearts and souls and spirits and lives
have been censored by mainstream off-the-shelf everything
and who were given instead the concrete void of insulin
metrazol electricity
hydrotherapy, psychotherapy
ping-pong & amnesia

oops, now, how did that line get in there?
how come nothing in the great american poetry anthology
reads like the america I know?
or sounds like the chrome tipped
cherry-bombed idle of a lowered *bomba* at the stoplight
with a tattered page manuscript
lying under a pile of sorry assed
thank you for your interest
rejection letters carpeting the floor?

IV.

Sometimes whenever my mom and I are going

down the road she'll see a television satellite dish

in someone's yard and say, "There's another home where

the woman has hung up her pan." We'll drive by

someone else's yard with another dish and she'll say,

"That's another house where the woman has

stopped feeding her family, not food, but stories."

—Sunny Dooley, Diné storyteller

Carmen Tells a Story

at the women's college
every Sunday we would sit and talk
about who we were
and where we were from

beautiful African women
stoic, strong

clikt, clikt, clikt
African chants, leopard scarves

a part of the earth, the women, as I
me, having come from a dirt road town
no road signs
community
familia
our life

this block to the end of the block
and all the people in between

the *tíos* and the *tías*

that which gave me life
Rock Springs, Wyoming
aquella otra vida
esta vecindad
iron caldron
comida del campo

I recall those kinds of things

Christmas
little red hearts
little treasures
nosotros, las hijas de Mares

outfits, dresses for us four daughters
misa del gallo
pan del horno
midnight mass

our father very often being gone
my mother, a maid
the convent housekeeper

one cow
one pig
gallinas
nos mandaban a ordeñar las vacas

bringing the cows home in the evening

we just knew
knew our cow
everyone knew their cow

Santistevan St.
'mana Felia
'mano Gabriel
los John Telles
the Trappers

one community

I received a scholarship to attend a women's college
¡iii!, I thought
¿qué andas haciendo mujer,
quieres ir, de veras quieres ir?

¡sí!

bueno, they told me, *tu abuelo te dará la bendición*
lo que pasa, pasa
you can always come home

me dieron la bendición
y me fui

blessed by the elders
and there we went, my friend and I
Carmen and Queenie
on a train bound for Loveland, Ohio

getting better was okay
not with a lot of words
but with approval
the reflection of my face
on the train's windowpane
¡eee, esta mujer!

leaving with trepidation
we were socially unadjusted, unbroken
what it meant to be in their world
Irish nuns

I remember coming back
twenty-five, twenty-six years old
la gente hablando, saying
¿cuándo se va a casar?

time was passing
in terms of my community

but, traveling was in my blood
maybe stayed in Taos a little bit longer
than I should've
I'm sure there's a good reason for that

everything was connected in our world
cows, manure
barking, visitors
we ate our own animals

mamá Carmelita
rece por nosotros

yerbas para resfríos
atole, chimajá, cota, yerba del manso

at the women's college
first year, second year
the lights alone
overwhelming
unlike back home, nature
infiltration
we, too, followed the migrant trail

she's Japanese, she's Hawaiian
where is she from?
everyone tried to guess
where everyone else was from

¡esos pendejos no saben!
why don't they know?
I thought

¿por qué no saben quién soy?

grandfather went to the Pueblos
to learn how to garden

I believed that tears were healthy
so I cried a lot

I would scream and howl
'cause the sorrow was so deep

200 acres, a new field of emotions
swaying like a cornfield in afternoon breeze

her *hijas* stayed secure
four daughters accompanied by *pachucos en* Taos
L O V E tattooed on the finger
a cross, a set of initials

and at the women's college there were
the hanging-loose-ones
but, no one making judgments
everyone had their own story

we give each other space
cross over each other's borders
song, dance, music
Philippine women
drums, silk,
lamb on Sunday

we put our *frijolitos* together
thirty years ago now, is it forty?

¡ay, Dios mío, cómo cambean las cosas
el tiempo se pasa. Dios mío!

As They Say Back Home

Nowadays news of a death
Comes easy

The phone rings
And you know it then

Through the familiar voice of that cousin
Who only calls when there's news
Of a certain magnitude

*¿¡quién, como, cuando, donde,
deveras!?*

Well, you know
I was just thinking about him
Yesterday, I think it was

Already the young fruit trees
In the front yard need pruning
And I was thinking
Wouldn't it be nice if he'd show up?

I'd pull out the shears
Afterwards, treat him to lunch
And some beers

I don't know why
But just yesterday
I was thinking about him

And I even laughed
Remembering his funny ways

I guess on his way out
He stopped by

Nagged me about the trees
Made me laugh

Easy come, easy go

What they say back home
It's understood, you know

Without any explanation

Nowadays news of a death
Comes easy

*In memoriam: Jon Garrifo,
tree pruner extraordinaire
y vato basilón*

El vecino

el vecino se arrima al cerco y me pregunta que si qué estoy haciendo
cuidado, no te vaya dar un heart attack, está muy caliente, me dice

es el mes de mayo y yo todavía ando peleándole a las charrangas
y él con su ranchito que *shinea* como un espejo

¿va haber agua? le pregunto, como él es de los hombres de edad y mure sabio
izque sí, dicen que sí

no, cuando hay agua vale nada, dice el vecino
el año pasaò estábamos regando a las dos de la mañana

ansina 'sta pelón, no se mira la agua, luego no corre
pero dicen que izque todavía hay nieve pa la Jicarita

¿y sus arboleras, allá bajo, dan fruta? le pregunto
viendo que su arbolerita está bien trimiadita como un *haircut* de peso

pues, tengo unos árboles de durazno—esos sí dan
¡o, dan unos duraznos como una béisbol!

no, dice el vecino, *estos árboles míos no dan fruta, ya 'stan muy viejos,*
eluego hela temprano. de este lado del río es muy helador

pa ya, pa La Otra Banda, sí se da manzana, pero de este lado, neh
una que otra, si no se la come el gusano o la echa a perder el granizo

el sol ya va a media mañana y nos despidemos
él a su negocio, y yo al mío

bueno, ahi nos 'stamos viendo
bueno, me dice el vecino, *muncho cuidao,*
ponte sombrero, no te vaya picar el sol

Dance of the Hollyhock

the morning's breeze this morning
blows with an air that is not summer
the first indication of fall
this other season already charcoaled
memories charred and singed
left over for another day
to be looked back upon in wonder,
the kind of wonder that offers an answer
only momentarily satisfying
as we move on, knowing that the palm heat of plenty
at times burns with the cold hand of not enough

but what is enough of anything, anymore?
so I offer you these words
on your upcoming birthday
because you have stood against
the flame and the wind,
have burnt your own candle down

and who should ask what light into what darkness
it may have lit
whose path it may have made all the easier for traveling
how much stronger the flicker at every breath
that threatened its radiance
when it danced alone
the bee's melody, the delightful drumming
of a soul beating with a heart of its own
the hummed song of summer from your mouth,
the pinkest flame licking upward

Corner of 5th & Central

my name is Kevin
rhymes with heaven
I'm the most photographed
homeless man in town

contrary to what
the bible thumpin' Jesus servants
told me

I am not lost

I am on the corner of 5th & Central
albuquerque, new mexico
united states of america
northern hemisphere

the planet is divided up into four quadrants

how I got started carving?

well, it was on a Sunday afternoon
it was raining
nothin' on TV
couldn't go fishin'

started poking around
the basement
found a ½" chisel
and a piece of wood

next thing I know
I'm looking at a fish

I got nothin' better to do
'cept think
and that's the one thing
they don't want you to do

you know that *TIME Magazine* thing,
greatest man of the century?
well, my question of the century is
if having more is so great
why aren't more people smiling?

I don't call this work
I call it love
'cause I love what I do

what good did fame and wealth do John F. Kennedy Jr.?
money don't mean shit
when you hit the water at 180 miles an hour

it pays for a good funeral
but, hell, you ain't there anyways

well, you come back

I'll tell you my whole life story
in about thirty seconds

El corrido de Arturo Romero

nacido el veintinueve de Mayo
en el año mil novecientos trece
le dice Juan Andrés a Juanita, *este hijo*
que Dios nos ha dado lo llamaremos Arturo,
¿Qué te parece?

entre los ojitos y los arroyitos de aquel valle conocido
como el Puesto del Embudo de San Antonio
entre sus mayores y la sabiduría del pueblo
donde con los truenos de marzo renace el retoño
allí fue Arturito creciendo

eran cinco de hermanos y hermanas carnal
Alfonso el abogado y Carlota la que vivía en Las Vegas
también la Marcia y la Leonardita que se casaron
con dos hermanos, Miguel y Ramón Casías
y el más conocido que fue su hermanito
el maestro de Dixon, Elías

en la escuela pronto aprendí a leer y a escribir
pero la verdad es, y ya saben que no estoy mintiendo
platicaba tío Arturo munchos años después
lo poquito que sé, en los campos lo fui aprendiendo

vestido en pecheras y con aquella risita, proclamaba
yo también fui al colegio pero trabajito
de corbata no fue para mí
a mí siempre me gustaron los animales
y la carrera de ranchero es la que yo descojí

en mi manera propia le doy gracias a Dios por su bendición
pero aunque mi tío Tomás fuera ministro, fe no le tengo a la religión
y a los doctores menos confianza les tengo
y de lo que me aconsejan calladito nomás me les río
allí en el cuartito tengo un saquito de remedios
para cuando se me atrinque el resfrío

ya ves esa mujer, decía tío Arturo con sus ojos brillando
esa es, esa es tu tía Celeste
ella es la que me cuida y por ella es que sigo viviendo
al Señor le pido que hasta el fin de mi vida Él me la preste

allí en aquella casita en Velarde
agachaban la cabeza en la mesa
con un ofrecimiento de gracias por su bien-estar
y a cualquier vesitante les decía tía Celeste
lávense las manos y arrímense
de esta casa nadien se va sin cenar

aquellos hombrecitos que criamos yo y tu tía,
Richard, Billy, y Carlitos, de ellos hablaba tío Arturo
con orgullo y amor ardiente
los amamos como nuestros propios hijos
pero pobrecitos los trabajamos como hombres
desde que eran chiquitos

un hombre fiel que no andaba con achaques ni excusas
si no estaba en su casa era que Arturo andaba dándole vuelta
a sus vacas en su querido rancho en las Tusas
en su profundo modo de primero observar y luego enseñar
una tarde que anduve con él, se me arrimó con una pacencia y me dijo
a estas criaturas no les tienes que gritar, no son como alguna gente, hijo
que estas solas entienden por donde salir y por donde entrar

el juicio de los hombres sabios
ya se nos está acabando, plebe
de eso no mienten mis labios
aquí termino, aquí ya me despido
con este homenaje a un hombre humilde y sencillo

un recuerdo también por sus queridos rancheros
de toditos estos valles hasta la más alta sierra
un gran saludo a todos ellos
eso es lo que Arturo pidiera

extranjero

and what are the names
in the envelopes that're
stuck still further inside the
bigger envelope?

and whose face
name
sound of voice

will each one belong to
who, who, is who?

the click of china

the soft touch of pen
red ink

the bird's chatter

it is in the blood

and the sameness

ritual

this old familiar town feeling to me strange

where are Orlando, Chris,
and Melvin, the R.D.T. boys
los vatos de Ranchos

all that then
all those other years
where?

the open flap, unlicked envelope
of the new and the now
takes its immediacy
and I've been having visions

cemetery crosses
off the road to El Prado

edgeworn headstones
deep blue sky, chamisa
the cemetery near Talpa

is that what the famed Taos artists felt
when they first came here

the familiar strange?

Tiwa
Castellano
Coyote

sharp, ancient,
prickling barbed wire
a rusted bolt latch

gnarled, twisted, wire wrapped
around the gatepost

at breakfast this morning strangers sat together
told stories
shared bread

it might've been stranger still
to not partake

personal observations, thoughts
kept to the self
the edges softened

the years, history
piled like padded mounds of earth
and prayer

ragweed growing
amidst the flowering
graveyards

Mi jaulita de oro

aquí en el Hotel de Cortez
al punto del universo
Avenida Central
calle Hidalgo y La Reforma

¿hasta cuándo aguantará
mi pensar?

estos días tan lejos
y tan cerca de ti

mi amada

tú que sola tú
me has dado las alas
para volar

cómo vuelan los poetas
con alas quebradas
bajo la luz de luna
en tierras ajenas

aquí, mil millas lejos de ti
me envuelvo en los perfumes
de tu vida y la mía

memorias distantes y acercadas
flores de jardín ajeno

querida esposa
ángel y bendición

yo sin ti fuera nada

y tal que todavía
me busco y me encuentro
solitario entre las calles

extrañando miradas de extranjeros
que alcanzarán ver a un hombre
como pajaro perdido

con alas quebradas
volando tope a tope

tan lejos y
tan cerca
de ti

Juxtaposition

throughout the years I have designed
high-end custom homes
crafting spatial poetics with *vigas* and *latillas*
hand peeled by *mojados*
whose sweat translates into profit for developers
working at a nifty rate

sometimes I go visit these homes
as they are being finished

may I help you?
I am asked by the realtor
standing at the door,
thinking that I may be the guy
who mixed the mud and pushed the wheelbarrow

I introduce myself as the designer

oh, well, it's so nice to meet you,
what a wonderful job!
please, come in.

I once was asked by a home magazine journalist
if I felt insulted by such incidents
well, no, I said, my mind mixing for an answer
a good batch of cement is never accidental

last year on my way up through Santa Fe
I made a detour and drove by a house of my design
the season's first snow on the ground,
smoke rising out of the fireplace chimney

inch by inch
I know that house
through its X, Y and Z axis

but, I cannot approach the front door
knock and expect to be invited in
to sit in the corner of my pleasing
and lounge around with the owner
as we sip on cups of hot herbal tea
making small talk about the weather
or discussing a reading
by the latest author come through
as the sun's last light
streams in gallantly
through the window
just where I placed it
and for that reason

I take a handful of snow to my mouth
toss another into the air
my blessing upon the inhabitants
que Dios los bendiga y les dé más
my grandfather would have said

I turn my car toward home
to my mother's house
a place near and far to me

she, my mother, is bedridden
and my brother is the self-appointed caretaker
to bathe her and feed her
bring her morsels of conversation

it is their own world now

ruled by a juxtaposition of understanding
against what I have come to know, now
here, so far and away

I am greeted at her front yard
by an old, propped up truck hood
proclaiming my brother's spray-painted inscription
    Jesus Saves
on the opposite side it reads
    Keep Out!

I guess it just depends on
what kind of day he's having,
someone once remarked
like a rattlesnake
it's a fair warning

years ago I accepted this madness
and called it not my own
it's better that he be drunk on Christ, said my mother
than on what he used to drink

we all agreed

Juan Sings Us

Las Mañanitas

on Easter Eve
I was at Carlos Chavez's
Juan's *compadre's* Easter *matanza*

a pig slaughter

and we get drunk
and stoned and we sing
and dance *rancheras*
around the fire

Juan sings me *Las Mañanitas*

the birthday morning
break of dawn
wake up serenade blessing
King David singing song

images of birds
and the music of heaven
San Juan y San Pedro

three weeks later
Juan leads our Jewish Seder in closing

his first Seder ever

with us all
all forty-five of us singing *Las Mañanitas*
at the table
cheering and crying

real salty tears
not plastic bowls of salty water
to dip our parsley into

no bitter horseradish
from jars at the end

no next year
in Jerusalem

no one future
all futures
right here
right now

Albuquerque, New Mexico
Pesach, 5757

estas son las mañanitas
que cantava el Rey David

hoy por ser día
de tu santo

te las cantamos
a ti . . .

for Mark Rudd
y
Juan in-a-million Saavedra

Yellow

the color yellow
in the way the word reflects

the written line is simply that
a line, a bead of light

wordless

colored against the silence
of the walls

and the phone ringing in the adjacent room

these tables and the flicking of pens
across the paper

we are so used to what we have
drying in, drying out

what brings me here
a ray of hope
at summer's end

glowing with a dimness flat and pale
against a fullness formed of nothing

each other's lives
backgrounds
what we
do

who we are
in becoming, now

is it enough to feel
comfortable, to trust?

we are so used to what we have

that in the letting go
one often stumbles

would you pick me up, really?
or reach out?

your pure reaction
balancing my shoulder, easing my fall

your words there to hold me

she said the chair had flipped out from under her
as she cleaned out the cupboards
while the girls were in the tub
and what if she had hit her head against the tile counter
or the washing machine?
the thump of skull
against the metal

i can hear it now

the wooden chair legs
scraping across the floor
an arc, swift in its pivotal transition

we are so used to what we have,
yet, always reminded of *what ifs*

what if she had been knocked unconscious
with the girls in the tub
and the phone ringing

my call to see how things were going

the light glowing thick and dim
another transition in our lives

outside, August and the sunset dancing
the afternoon's plucked sunflowers on the table

if you look deep into their center
i mean deep, really deep

you can see freshly plowed fields
going on forever
or, maybe, just simply
something that reminds you of something
like coffee grains

we are so used to what we have
that much goes unnoticed
unsaid

thoughts turned on-n-off

the color yellow
in the way the light reflects
and our lives
wordless under it all

the morbidity is set before us
not lengthwise
but perpendicular to the crooked line
like old adobe

the light, yellow and wavering

V.

It is a poetry of remembrance

and of an honoring of land and people

earth songs, love poems

born of celebration and mourning

A Poetry of Remembrance

it may be

the sky
its evening color
just north on the horizon lifting
in whispers
of apricot, lavender, and periwinkle

or it may be

the way the old rusted cars' rooftops
smudge into the solemn landscape's drifting light
cartwheeling across the alfalfa field
towards a full moon in coming

i am sure it is that
this evening

which makes it difficult
for us to gather our bags
and continue on

even though
we have garnished what we can
and like a grandmother's measure
take with us
no more and no less

here
aquí en este pueblo
en este valle
en esta vecindad

it is a poetry of remembrance
and of an honoring of land and people

earth songs
love poems
born of celebration and mourning

in the place where I come from

> *también de gusto se llora*
> *como de tristeza se canta*

and under that colorful backdrop
of a spring dusk framing the village

there are sad stories
that bind us in our comings
there are joyful stories
that bind us in our goings

at times we see
a finality to a way of life no longer
but we carry in our hearts
a memoried time the *ancianos* speak of

through the poetry
and the song and the rhythm
of their stories

　　and we take their stories
　　and we form ours to theirs
　　and we lament the tongue
　　recalling the sound
　　of its native language

　　how we carry it with us
　　into this, our other world
　　lamenting the spirit of the heart
　　which will cry out to no one's hearing

　　and we take the forewarning of the elders
　　and we'll remember, we'll remember, we'll remember

　　and we'll laugh and join
　　in the circle of our brethren
　　in that vast periphery
　　hollow and echoing
　　remembering us home

　　because we are still alive

　　and we'll rejoice and feast
　　in the clumsiness of our faith
　　and we'll dance around the open fire
　　stepping out into the next tomorrow

because we are still alive
because we are still alive
because we are still alive

or maybe

it's simply the thump
of the trunk lid as it is shut
the one more final good-bye having been said
the family dog gone wagging its way
back under the old retired family sedan

Venus already twinkling

it may be that
this evening

which makes it difficult
for us to gather ourselves
and continue on

Corrales de Vadito

en un parqueadero al lado del camino
allí nos entreteníanos
matando el rato

así me detuve esta mañana
y me rolié un papelito de punchi
y luego le seguí al camino

allí venía atrás de un Peñasquero
que traiba su troca bien cargada

leña de otoño

un pasteo con vacas

las acequias

el Río Pueblo

los corrales de Vadito

me acordé de ti
hermano
y me suelté llorando

el radio tocando
traición y el contrabando

escribí estas líneas
en una servilleta manchada

¿cómo fueran sido los años?

un ranchito

un hatajito de vacas

paseándote por la pareja
en un alazán a pelo

tu cría juegando en el arroyo
creciendo como la yerba
entre las cuatro milpas

nada más quedó
sólo recuerdos

una cruz al lado del camino
tu nombre sobrepintado

entramos al otoño, hermano
sin tu música
sin el sonido de tu guitarra
sin oír tu voz raspando

entramos a la media vuelta
escuchando solamente

los tristes grillos de Agosto

De donde yo soy

I am from leche de jarro
from Morrell manteca and Gold Medal flour
I am from acequias, viviendas, dispensas, y
el Rosario recited on Radio *¿Qué Dice?*
I am from the irises drooping like teardrops
in grammita's abandoned flower bed
y las Varas de San José
whose long gone limbs I remember
as if they were my own

I'm from ojos verdes and travesuras y avergonzadas
from mis primos Peter and Jondas de La Villita
I'm from *no friegues con migo* and *que Dios te bendiga*
from *dime con quíen andas y te diré quíen eres*
I'm from *¡pórtate bien, repártete con tu hermano*
y no seas malcriado!

I am from Santos, velas, and *lo que será, será*
I am from aquel vallecito de lágrimas
soy de Romero, Atencio, Valdez, y Durán
vengo de *hablan cuando no deben de hablar*
y son callados cuando deben de decir algo
soy de atole, frijolitos, papas con carne, y chile colorado
from *tu abuelo, Juan Andrés, murió en la borrega en Monte Vista*
y tu otro abuelo, Silviares, viajaba vendiendo fruta
desde el Embudo hasta Ratón

los retratos de mis antepasados
los traigo en mi corazón
yo soy un manito del Norte
me río por no llorar
soy de aquel mestizaje floreciendo
como el rocío en el amanecer

thin nickel

my eight-year-old daughter
is beginning to worry me
she is apt to call tacos, *burritos*
frogs, *fish*, cows, *horses*

I don't know who she gets that from
it must be her mother
who calls me *faithful*
and a *good provider*
even calls me *level headed*

I whose true love and dedication
is this other one called *Devotion*
sometimes goes by the name of *Passion*

that other one who stirs me up out of bed
at whatever hour of the night

so I can sit yanking at my hair
tending to these poems that never seem
to bring in a dime

Sunny Brook

it's all sorta here and there
and kinda hard to put into place
these stories that are bound to other stories

just last week on a quick trip back home
I met up with a friend from way back when
and he was hanging out
with some English-speaking, teasing, crazy *vatos*
on the eve of the Fourth of July

down at the river
near San Juan Pueblo
at a place they call Sunny Brook

Falcon Eddie was doing
just what he was doing
the last time I saw him
all those years ago

Eddie talkin' crazy talk

something 'bout the color of Indian skin
beautiful, just like that, he said
reaching out to touch
a San Juan Pueblo man's arm

hey, don't get me dirty!
says the guy to Falcon
and quickly brushes his hand away

Falcon's hands and fingers
black and oily from the transmission
he'd been working on for several days

And everyone laughs, jeering, hoofing, and hollering
the sunlight cascading through the cottonwoods
the river's sheet of water gently rippling by
the marooned tree trunks on the sandbar

Falcon
      the bros
            freedom
what's your name, bro? Falcon asks him

Daddy, Big Daddy, your papa, 'ey

and we laugh some more
to Big Daddy and Falcon Eddie and the bros
on Independence Weekend

down at the river
near San Juan
at a place they call
Sunny Brook

and freedom
what freedom?
someone remarks
hell, you can't even drink a beer anymore!

and everyone reaches down to retrieve
their beers after thinking
the last car going by might've been a cop

and me and my
      I gotta go
       I can't stay long
         wish I could
           but, I have to get back home
            and work tomorrow

you gotta work tomorrow?
  tomorrow's Saturday!

the questions flare
      it's the Fourth of July weekend, man!

yeah, yeah, I know, but . . .

and freedom, what freedom?

I hear their laughter
and that question for miles
and days into the years
of a long road maybe someday
bringing me back to Falcon Eddie, Big Daddy
and the bros

down at the river
near San Juan
at that place they call
Sunny Brook

columpio

i feel like i'm finally getting back
into the swing of things

the trees not yet begun to lose their
leaves
i too
am static as the

right before

i watch the cat's hair
on its back
bristle

a sun-ripened season
a stray dog on a stroll
autumn's light and shadow
crickets eulogizing summer

the *vecina* said
she had been canning apples this past week
baking pies, churning apple butter
and hanging up time

on the clothesline

yesterday afternoon
i met a man
walking along the ditch bank

unshaven and thickly bundled
for mid-september, i thought,
from his fingers hung
a can of beer

¿qué andas haciendo? he asked
buscando la llorona, i said
¿no la has visto?

he smiled
a flash of beautiful
false teeth
his eyes dark as walnuts

ni la conozco, he said
denying everything

i saw the reflection of my shadow
floating down the acequia

a tire half buried in the mud
with a broken

rope snaking
in the
weeds

La fijancia es la mala

la Esther
la Albinita
y la Linda

chavalas traviesas
del barrio aquel de mi
tierra negra

de arroyos, arboleras, alfalfas,
zacates, acequias, caminitos de tierra

barrio de carrilla
y de carrilla de a madre

sobrenombres, lenguas sueltas
repicando como capanas rechinozas

¡órale, fregasos, en donde sea
a mí se me hace nada!

peleoneros, babosos, aprovechados
que hicieron corazónes sufrir

hoy soy el hombre fuerte
que soy

por mal que me trataron

pero, no hay pedo
como dijo Socrates,

yo no quiero pleito

malditos maestros
con los brazos cruzados
que nos toreaban a pelear

años despues
hoy yo también

me curo

carrilla amuelada apuntando
al mero cora'
borrándose ya en el librito negro
pájinas sueltas en un
viento armargozo

¿Y, Quién Es Tu Daddy?

tío mato, choche, chivato, la peca,
los tofes, los toros, los changos, indio,
perro flaco, la pimpora, el piñón, el borreguita,
chango malo, la justicia, juan moco, juan mudo,
juan dormido, la betty bubbles, el gorgojo,
el perico, el beef, manuel pato, los mopes,
pinochio, el cartucho, chihuahuita, el parranditas,
franque llorón, banano, la choriza, los mocosos,
el magoo, el quara, el vaquero, el chuple,
el choque, el jombo, zorrillo, la vetalla,
los cotencios, tone gato, el pichel, el tamalero,
el diablo, la bruja, el chamín turtle

¡ay,
no se agüiten,
nomás monqueando!

años después

hoy yo también

me curo

Taos Nicho

¿tus santos y tus velas
qué me salvarán?

sin la cruz
no hay gloria

pero como dice mi Hermano Juan
  todos quieren la gloria
  pero nadien quiere la cruz

indigenous mother
encased in the dead dust
of permanence

how fast the world
  goes us by
shadowy and flapping
like the clothes on the line
  in the backyard
  off a backroad
  in Ranchos

the sky darkening
along the edge of the mountain
autumn storm clouds approaching

slowly

as if set and framed within
a landscape interpretation
of an oil or pastel

to what direction
  should i cast out my prayers?

the sun comes up still
    to the east

but my life is disoriented

my feet are fast and swift

but with no direction
no intent, other than
in the getting there

i feel like the Indian dancer
in the painting
whose headdress and plumes
are frozen
    and whose gaze
        has been blushed out
            by a well applied
                brushstroke

it is in the what
    is not there
        that one can find what is

on this day, *en este día*
    el Día de La Asunción de Nuestra Señora

i watched footage
of last summer's parade
on the local TV station

watched the young fiesta queen
    white gloved and crowned
        waving her hand
            flicking her wrist
                in perfect motion

to the crowd along
the procession
as they do
in events and places like Macy's
or Pasadena

and the young caballeros
on their stout horses
trailed behind

yelling through perfect teeth
  ¡Que Viva la Fiesta!

dressed as Conquistadores
wearing their new grown beards
and the latest style of sunglasses

and i thought of the Pueblo down road

and what its people
must feel for this
      reenactment

and i am everything at that point

    and nothing

for i could feel joyous and celebratory
for we have endured

my people
mi raza
el mestizaje

la huerfandad

the orphaned ones

whom Spain abandoned
Mexico did not adopt
and the U.S. never wanted

and i feel the sorrow of the *Indio*

because of that
        enduring

and my heart
    if it could be captured
        painted and displayed
            exhibited in the finest gallery
                where the locals do not enter

would be earthen, grayed
and splintered
a tinge of red perhaps
colors of
        the wooden crosses

tilting in their final balance

in the *camposanto*
        among the ruins
        of that first *iglesia*

destroyed in the Pueblo Revolt
        of that not
        so long
        ago

Molino abandonado

sopla viento, sopla más
y la paja volará
ahi preparado el banquete
pa' todo el que vaya entrando

sopla viento, sopla más
y la paja volará
ahi preparado el banquete
pa' todo el que vaya entrando

la historia
de un pueblo

hecha polvo

¿qué pasó aquí,
qué es esto?

¿en dónde está la sabiduría
granma, granpa?

ya no quedan ni mígajas
ni tansiquiera una tortilla dura

¿el sonido esta tarde?

una *Harley* retumbando por la plaza
¿y con eso seponemos de quedar contentos?

sopla viento, sopla más
y la paja volará
ahi preparado el banquete
pa' todo el que vaya entrando

sopla viento, sopla más
y la paja volará
ahi preparado el banquete
pa' todo el que vaya entrando

aquel molino
en un tiempo con su rueda en el agua
ahora, se usa de dispensa

¡ay, hasta miedo me da
arrimarme a este pueblo!
las lenguas como flechas
apuntadas y venenosas

somos hijos de los hijos
de hombres en aquel antepasado
que se trataban como hermanos
ayudándose unos a los otros
al estilo mano a mano

sopla viento, sopla más
y la paja volará
ahi preparado el banquete
pa' todo el que vaya entrando

sopla viento, sopla más
y la paja volará
ahi preparado el banquete
pa' todo el que vaya entrando

¿qué pasó aquí,
qué es esto?

¿qué no te conozco,
de qué familia eres?

¡o, pues, yo y tu abuelo anduvimos juntos
en la borrega en Colorado
y en el betabel en Wyoming!

nos conocemos bien
sin saber quién semos

esta tarde, aquí

el maíz bailando
seco en el viento

y el pueblo sin molino

sopla viento, sopla más
y la paja volará
ahi preparado el banquete
pa'todo el que vaya entrando

sopla viento, sopla más
y la paja volará
ahi preparado el banquete
pa' todo el que vaya entrando

Note: Repeating chorus is taken from a traditional canto, *"trillando*—el trill." It was used at the community *molino* in the village of Apodaca, New Mexico, as crops such as corn, beans, chile, or wheat were laid out and sifted in *sábanas* in the afternoon breeze to remove dust and debris before grinding. The *canto* was handed down to me by Aaron Griego. In conjunction with the first reading of the poem, the *canto* was sung for the first time in over fifty years by Vicente Griego, flamenco cantador, in Needleboro, Maine, as part of Robert Bly's Seventh Annual Conference on the Great Mother and New Father. *pa que sepan y chepan~*

"a person is not truly dead
until their name is no longer
spoken or remembered"
—Quién Sabe Quién

El veintinueve de agosto
me acuerdo como si ayer fuera

comienzo con la fecha del día
porque así es como se acuerdan
los ancianos de los tiempos

de los tiempos
buenos
de los tiempos
malos

¿cómo estás, Mom?

bien, lo mismo, aquí
no te conocí
pensé que eras un americano

my mother lies in bed
fondles the sheets stiffly
with her gnarled fingers

rheumatism
and now it's come down to this

a nursing home

the scent of ammonia and urine
mingling like rival companions
each one commanding
territorial rights over the other

my mother questions me
asks me about people whom I've never met

some who died even before I was born
I think, not because
she could be suffering slightly from dementia

but because that is our enduring history

so that those people

their names
their peculiarities
their characteristics
their quirks
their lives
are still vital
even now

someone quoted over breakfast
yesterday morning
what someone had said about small towns
and people

you can't take away their gossip,
it's all they have

my mother carries on
her stories and observations

gossip based on truth
and truth formed of speculation

and although the rumors
the stories
the gossip
are public knowledge
over forty years old

I cringe to think
what if someone heard

and, Mom, where did I get my name from?

oh, well, you know
you were named after your cousin,
but his godmother who gave the name to him
well, you know how she was

she gave him that name because she said,
she said that his father wasn't his real father
and so she gave him that name
you know, just to be like that

you know how she was, remember?

well, no, Mom, I think to myself
I never knew her

and I lean forward
closer in to her voice
into the story

hoping that no one else will hear
although those people

the father, my cousin, and the woman
who baptized him
the others

they are all passed away now

and still the stories are spoken
as if they matter
as if the knowing means something

I mention to my cousin that my mother
is beginning to tell me the same stories
over and over again

she doesn't want you to forget them! he insists

   oh, and your tía
   she used to be so jealous
   of my brother

I remember one time
when he was getting ready to go out
to sell fruit and vegetables
and, oh, how she didn't want him to go
you know?

she didn't want him to go into the other towns
meet other women

I was just a small girl then
but she had me help her that morning
and, oh, how she made me carry those watermelons
for what seemed like hours

and we'd carry them
and drop them into the outhouse
so that there'd be less produce for your tío to take

oh, I remember your tía

you remember how she was!
remember?

and that is how we remember

and the stories are spoken
as if they matter

as if the knowing means something

so that
those people

their names
their peculiarities
their characteristics
their quirks
their lives
remain vital
through the then
through the now

   ¡acuérdate, mi 'jito!

remember!

Afterword

WE ARE PLEASED TO INCLUDE Levi Romero's *A Poetry of Remembrance: New and Rejected Works* in the Pasó por Aquí series as part of our commitment to publishing new fiction and poetry by Hispanic New Mexican writers while we continue to recover the Nuevomexico literary tradition of the past four centuries. Romero's extraordinary poetry falls very much within our purview of gathering the literature, art, and culture of Hispanic New Mexico now so as not to have to recover it later. Indeed, by publishing contemporary cultural production we are recovering the future.

Levi Romero possesses a poetic sensibility that is deeply intelligent in describing the nature of experience and consciousness, whether that be in the profound awareness embedded in the most common perception of everyday life or when considering the kinds of life-modifying experiences that trouble us to understand our griefs, joys, and rare moments of self-recognition, notwithstanding our cultural differences. Romero's poetry is so carefully crafted that it teaches us all to see more precisely, to think more expansively, and to feel more deeply, and Romero achieves this complex effect through a poetics that is the more powerful for being so often understated.

A poem like "Dance of the Hollyhock" is a wonderfully understated, or actually unstated, meditation on the small actions in the natural world that remind us of ourselves, that make us more fully alive to the experience of seeing. "Yellow" is a sharp articulation of self-consciousness and the ways in which we are "so used to what we have" that alternate "what ifs" or near accidents jolt us out of complacency, if only momentarily, with the kind of momentary force that creates both fear of what might have just happened or, more painfully, what often waits to happen. And it is in that momentary "what if" that the reader stops to catch his breath and sigh relief for the small blessings we enjoy.

The lyrics of personal experience alternate with poems that are set in the large social and economic structures that trouble everyday life. In "Juxtaposition," for example, the speaker is an architect "crafting spatial poetics with *vigas* and *latillas*," often mistaken for "the guy/who mixed the mud and pushed the wheelbarrow." When he drives by a home of his design in Santa Fe, he knows that he cannot

knock and expect to be invited in
to sit in the corner of my pleasing
and lounge around with the owner
as we sip on cups of hot herbal tea
. . . discussing a reading
by the latest author come through
as the sun's last light
streams in gallantly
through the window
just where I placed it
and for that reason.

Finally, a few words on the centerpiece of the collection, "Low-cura," a narrative meditation on lowrider culture in Española that Romero refers to as an "American subcultural tradition." This piece combines poetry and lyrical prose, personal, familial, and cultural history to produce a narrative not only about Chicano car culture, but about American commodity culture, intercultural history, language variation, and social exclusion. The scenes here are always at work in the language, images, and metaphors of Romero's careful craft, sometimes heard in the direct articulations of his characters and just as often in the substructures of feeling and perception. The narrative voices often float between English and New Mexican Spanish, or the easy bilingual fusion of the two languages, and in such poems language itself is a metaphor for the history of cultural practice, whether imaged as a "bumper scraping cruiser" or poetry about who owns poetry:

how come nothing in the great american poetry anthology
reads like the america I know?
or sounds like the chrome tipped
cherry-bombed idle of a lowered *bomba* at the stoplight
with a tattered page manuscript
lying under a pile of sorry assed
thank you for your interest
rejection letters carpeting the floor?

Levi Romero's is a poetry profoundly about the Chicano culture of New Mexico, alive in every line to the complexity of experience as it ranges from intimate personal and domestic feeling to engagement with the great social, linguistic, and political issues of the day. Yet, it is a poetry that speaks to the experience of feeling, seeing, and being alive that we all experience. We are very excited to have *A Poetry of Remembrance: New and Rejected Works* placed in the Pasó por Aquí series.

—Genaro M. Padilla
For the Pasó por Aquí editors

Acknowledgments/Reconocimientos

I am indebted to audiences, readers, writers' programs, literary arts organizations, directores y directoras, estudiantes, amistades, *and all who supported my work as a writer and instructor these last 10,000 miles or so. To note one risks leaving someone else out* y con eso les doy mis sinceras gracias a cada uno y todos. *With all love, respect, and admiration for* Sandra Cisneros, maestra, hermana, visionaria. En reconocimiento también a mi familia literaria del Macondo Writers' Workshop. Con aprecio a Shelle Sánchez, Jesus "Chuy" Martínez, y Mikaela Renz-Whitmore *for their dedication to the literary arts as a form of artistic liberation and for providing positive, life-shaping environments for the youth and writers of all ages and backgrounds.* Un abrazo de caridad a los Hermanos y Hermanas de la Morada de San José de Alburquerque y a toda la Hermandad del suroeste. Saludes a mis amigos, parientes y vecinos de mi pueblo, Embudo, y a primo Alberto Lovato por sus consejos y pláticas, aunque esté más ocupáo que los perros y más loco que las cabras. También a Mark Rudd *for creating community, family, and teaching us acceptance, tolerance, and forgiveness.* Y un gran saludo a todos mis parientes y queridos 'manitos por allá en Wyoming, Colo, Utah, Nevada, Califa, y otros países and *to the new generation of* poetas y escritores dándole *shine* a la palabra; James, Kim, Damien, Carlos, Jessica, Jasmine, Adam, Hakim, y los demás *Spoken Word crafters* de 'Burque. Sin olvido, a la memoria de Raúl Salinas y la plebe de Resistencia Bookstore en Austin. Gracias a Yolanda Romero Jaramillo y Enrique Lamadrid por su asistencia editorial sobre el español. Y mis más profundas gracias a Dr. Tobías Durán por toda su *esquina* entre los años.

The following poems first appeared in these publications:

"Hearts and Arrows," "Los Heroes," "Wheels,"
and "Easynights and a Pack of Frajos" in
In the Gathering of Silence, West End Press

"Capulín" in *The Harwood Review*

"Dear Ullyses"
in *The Harwood Anthology,* Old School Books

"High School English" ("Inglés de la preparatoria," Spanish translation)
in *Revista Casa de Las Américas,* Havana, Cuba

"Lowcura: A *Virtual Cruise* Through an American Subcultural Tradition"
in *Lowrider: An American Cultural Expression,* the Smithsonian Institution

"New and Rejected Works" in
A Bigger Boat: The Unlikely Success of the Albuquerque Poetry Slam Scene,
The University of New Mexico Press

"extranjero" in *Reeds and Rushes: Pitch, Buzz, and Hum,*
Pudding House Publications

"De donde yo soy" in *Dream in Color,* Scholastic

"Molino Abandonado"
in the New Mexico Office of the State Historian's
on-line literary map